HEY... FUTURE
REAL ESTATE AGENT

Your Strategic Guide
Into the Business and Beyond

Desireé L. Burgos

hello@bookedandbound.com
www.bookedandbound.com
209 Cooper Avenue, Ste. 8a, Montclair, NJ 07043

Version Note

This is the second version of *Hey...Future Real Estate Agent: Your Strategic Guide Into The Business And Beyond*. Minor updates have been made to Chapters 2, 3, and 8, which do not alter the overall message of the book. Additionally, this version features a new photo of the author on the back cover. The first version was published in February 2024, while the second version was published in November 2024.

Published by

Booked and Bound, LLC

209 Cooper Avenue, Montclair, New Jersey

hello@bookedandbound.com

www.bookedandbound.com

ISBN: 979-8-9898788-1-9

Library of Congress Control Number: 2024902293

Co-Illustrator

Andrew J. Burgos

Editor

Amya Zhanelle, MS

Photography

AZ Is Media

Disclaimer

This book is designed to provide accurate and authoritative information regarding the subject matter covered. It is sold with the understanding that the publisher and author, illustrator, or editor are not engaged in rendering legal, accounting, or other professional advice. If legal or expert assistance is required, the services of a competent professional should be sought.

Foreword

When I started my journey as a real estate agent over two decades ago, it was a haphazard beginning. I stumbled upon testing dates in a newspaper and joined a course on a whim. Initial training consisted of a shared phone, a phonebook, and a desk – it felt like a game of "Go Fish!"

Today, I stand in awe of Desireé L. Burgos' remarkable mentorship skills. In this book, her intelligence gleams as she goes beyond the allure of income potential, TV, and social media hype. She shares relatable stories from her entrepreneurial career and real estate journey, emphasizing action steps to led readers to sustainable success.

Desireé masterfully coaches aspiring real estate entrepreneurs and future agents, demystifying the licensing process and equipping them for success through her writing. While she may playfully acknowledge my role in her path to real estate and dually give my ego a high five, it's her innate ability, sheer knowledge, and passion for simplifying the path to success in achievable steps that form the core of this strategic guide for aspiring agents and brokers.

Whether you seek information or inspiration, this book is the ultimate go-to preparation guide for those considering a real estate career as an agent. As someone who lacked such a guide, I attest to its value. Now, as a seasoned real estate broker, I'm grateful that my personal SMART goals led me to marry the author of this invaluable resource and as a bonus, I have her insight on deck 24/7!

This book, titled "Hey...Future Real Estate Agent: Your Strategic Guide Into The Business and Beyond," is a testament to Desireé's dedication and expertise. I wholeheartedly recommend it to anyone on the path to a rewarding real estate career and business venture.

Joseph Burgos, Real Estate Broker

President and CEO

Burgos Realty Company®

Contents

Chapter One

Preparing to Become a Real Estate Agent

Are you considering a career as a real estate agent? Looking to build a small business as an agent in the industry or better yet, an empire? Well, let me assure you, real estate is an excellent choice! Not only can it be a financially lucrative business and profession, but it also provides significant flexibility and ample room for personal and professional growth. It's true, but not breaking news and that probably feels a little blah...blah...blah of an answer because this is something you assumed, right? And maybe, what you really want to know is if you can actually do this...right?

Listen, real estate is a hot...haute business venture, literally and figuratively, but can you handle that heat? Are you built for the fire this business brings? Like any business, there are many elements to learn and areas to broaden your knowledge base. Yet your ability to stand on top of the flames relies on you putting the consistent and strategic work in while igniting the power in the one thing that is already in you. Passion. So, let's get into it!

Embracing your passion for real estate forms the foundation of a thriving career as an agent and business. This fulfilling adventure commences with sincere joy for assisting individuals in discovering their ideal homes and or commercial spaces. There is a meaningful impact that comes from the work of a real estate agent. It's not your typical business. Lives are changed, generational wealth is enhanced, and overall legacies are built through the work we do. All while building strategic relationships, adding value, and maneuvering through the dynamic terrain of the real estate market.

The way you decide to lean into this industry as an agent will be the compass to your intrinsic fulfillment and business success. Authenticity is a necessity as it will straighten your lines and curve your edges as a checkpoint for the moment and your ultimate vision. Similarly, the continuous quest to learn how the real estate industry and the specific markets you serve, move is a strategic play that will induce boundless opportunities. While full confidence in your unique brilliance contrasted with hosting the emotional intelligence necessary for sufficient nimbleness to give and accept, will protect your business and your being when the turbulence of real estate and entrepreneurship delivers undesirable currents. The adoring landscape this business offers can shift like an abrupt force of nature lacking warning. Yet, fully understanding that your ultimate asset is the value you lead with, will empower your path and elevate your competitive advantage favorably--put on display attracting an abundance of worth, wealth, and wins.

The secret go-pro sauce is simple...

Learn continuously. Lead with undeniable value. Grow unapologetically. Repeat.

Can you do that?

A Piece of My Story

I've been where you are right now seeking information and resources on how to get started and sustain a successful real estate business as an agent. I tapped into every resource I had access to and could find. Fortunately for me, my husband was already a spicey, well-seasoned, top-producing and licensed Real Estate Broker. However, there were arcas, and specifically, because he knows how analytical I am, he would only make light suggestions and sometimes point me to various, (*more than I had time to review*), resources. My pain point arose mainly because much of the information, although useful, was disjointed, in different places--not centralized.

My abundant desire for information, based on the way I thought I'd operate and add value in this industry, for my clients, community, and business was expansive. I bet... in an overwhelming way--(ok, annoying) at times too – but don't tell my husband that I ever admitted that! Anyway, either because he was fully invested in my success, super excited about working together daily, or wanted to ensure that the arroz con habichuelas guisado or the baked mac and cheese and all of my culinary masterpieces didn't cease, he availed himself to answer my absolutely endless list of questions. Talk about leverage! During that time, having his almost half-century of real estate knowledge on deck (*I made him sound ancient, didn't I* ?) while getting started in this industry was and still is a useful resource. It's a privilege that I'm clear, many entrepreneurs seeking to leap into real estate don't have, which is the idea that birthed this book.

My questions spanned from...

- Where would I find a course or study program?
- Could I test out of the course requirement?
- What was the probability of passing the test in one shot? (that was a personal thing for me)
- How would I effectively manage time for this business with my already full plate?
- Which markets and niches should I focus on?
- How do I build an independent brokerage? (that was the direction for us)
- How I'd exceed my prior income and multiply it by half the year?
- If any part of the real estate business complimented my strategic goals?
- What if....???
- and on and on...

My questions were overflowing because real estate was a complete career shift, or better yet a dynamic overhaul for me and I was nervous--literally leaning into a new thing scared. So my pursuit for robust, make it make sense type of information, to find the comfort I believed I needed to efficiently leap into this space was more than abundant, to say the least. I'm pretty sure I'm not the only one and because of that assumption, I'm giving you all the intel you need to dive into this business BIG scared with clarity. Consider it your informational edge...minus the culinary effort or marriage vows to a real estate broker. See what I did there?

Before entering the real estate industry, I embarked on several diverse career paths and entrepreneurial opportunities. All of which enriched my value, broadened my knowledge, and positioned me well for where I am in business today. Many lessons from my earlier endeavors have proven to be highly relevant to my current roles as a licensed real estate agent and a multi-state real estate brokerage owner. In sync with God's timing, my husband "the Broker" was the catalyst for my leap into real estate. He had a 20+ year headstart in the industry when I finally said yes to partnering in his dream of building an independent real estate brokerage. Recognizing the potential for me to leverage my leadership experiences, relationships, and business development skills, I eventually decided to lean all the way in and pursue attaining a real estate license. That process alone unveiled to me, another layer about myself and how I'd eventually add value in this new space.

And so, here we are.

In each chapter throughout this book, you'll get to learn from my experience. I'll guide you through how to get started as a real estate agent and demystify the pre-licensing process required to sell real estate. I'll share some of my stories, the advantages of embarking on a career as a real estate agent, and pro tips to ultimately develop a profitable real estate business model within this fascinating industry. And since I love to give stuff away...be sure to grab the QR Code floating throughout this book to get access to some FREE-for-you downloads!

Chapter Two

The Bag and The Business

Money, money, money and more money...let's dive right into the earning potential and what the business will look like for the path you select.

"The Bag" aka Income

As a real estate agent, you possess the power to shape your financial prosperity according to your aspirations. Naturally, your potential earnings are influenced by various factors, such as the dynamics of your local market and how you strategically market your business. The types of properties you specialize in can also make an impact if your bag is absent or abundant. However, it's important to emphasize that the extensive earning potential in real estate is indeed available for you to seize upon your strategic, unrelenting diligence aka put the work in!

What sets the real estate industry apart from many other careers is the level of control you have over your income. In this profession, your efforts directly correlate with your earnings. In other words, the more properties you successfully sell, the more you stand to make and that part is subjective and I'll tell you why. You have to make your business model make sense. Ordering business cards and posting on social with cute outfits here and there is not going to fill your bag in any sustainable way. However, SMART strategy (which we'll get into in later chapters) will.

It might be surprising, but sometimes simple tweaks like reducing your volume and strategically targeting higher-priced markets can reap healthy returns. The reverse strategy is true for agents who have the ability to reach into untapped markets or those who resonate with a niche market that they have the skill set, will, and value to support. Your income isn't capped by a fixed salary *(unless you opted for the employee route)* but rather determined by your dedication, skills, willingness to learn, and the results you actually achieve. This means that with diligence, expertise, and effective sales strategies, you can steadily increase your income (fill your bag) and build the financially fulfilling career and business you desire.

So, if you're motivated by the prospect of earning potential that aligns with your ambition and effort, a career in real estate offers an exciting path to financial success aka "abundant bag".

We'll get into "the bag" more when we discuss expenses and budgeting your benjamins in a later chapter. Keep reading, but when you are ready to sort out your income and expenses, scan this QR code for a FREE 12-month template you can use to get started. Or...scan it right now so you don't forget and save it for later!

The Business View

Before we lean too deep into this book, it's important to note that as a real estate agent, you are the business. It's also essential for you to understand the definition and role of the different categories of real estate agent licensure. In the next few sections of this chapter, we will discuss the real estate agent, the referral agent, and the broker. Pay close attention because many states use the broker title for what other states call a real estate agent. Additionally, some states don't differentiate between the real estate agent and referral agent while others do.

And...just so there aren't any misunderstandings...know that you'll need to pass the national and state real estate exam for your selected state of licensure and attain a real estate license before you can act as a real estate agent or real estate broker in any state. You cannot represent others with their lease, purchase, or sale of real estate and receive a commission without a real estate license. More about study, schools, prerequisites, and the exam in later chapters.

Real Estate Agent

A real estate agent is a licensed professional who represents clients in real estate transactions. They play a vital role in the buying, selling, or renting of residential and commercial properties. Acting as intermediaries, the expertise of an agent helps clients navigate the complexities of the real estate market. Real estate agents have a fiduciary duty to act in their client's best interests, providing honest and ethical representation throughout the entire process. Remember that detail, you'll thank me later!

Agent responsibilities encompass various facets of the real estate journey. For buyers and tenants, agents assist in the property search by identifying options that align with their preferences, needs, and budgets. They leverage their knowledge of the real estate market to find suitable properties. On the other hand, for sellers and landlords, agents take charge of marketing properties to potential buyers or tenants. This involves creating property listings, staging homes, conducting open houses, and implementing advertising strategies to attract ready, willing, and able buyers.

Negotiation is a crucial aspect of their role, as real estate agents negotiate on behalf of their clients to secure the most favorable deals possible. They help clients make competitive offers or counteroffers and facilitate negotiations until mutually acceptable terms are reached. Extensive paperwork and documentation are handled by agents to ensure all legal documents, contracts, and disclosures are properly completed and filed.

Market knowledge is another key area of expertise for real estate agents. They stay informed about market trends, property values, and local regulations, offering valuable insights to clients for informed decision-making. Additionally, real estate agents are professionals who often have extensive networks within the real estate industry, including connections with other agents, lenders, inspectors, appraisers, and contractors. This network proves invaluable in facilitating transactions.

To maintain their licenses, real estate agents frequently participate in continuing education courses, ensuring they remain up-to-date on industry changes and best practices. Many of these continuing education courses are required in order for the agent to keep their license. However, agents have the option to elevate their value by participating in courses and achieving certifications and designations above and beyond requirements. While their core roles and responsibilities remain consistent, the specifics may vary depending on state regulations, as real estate practices and laws differ across jurisdictions.

Referral Agent

A real estate referral agent is a licensed real estate professional who primarily focuses on referring clients or prospective buyers and sellers to other real estate agents or brokers. Instead of actively representing clients in real estate transactions, a referral agent connects individuals interested in buying or selling property with experienced agents or brokers who can provide them with the necessary services and expertise.

The role of a real estate referral agent is to facilitate connections between clients and full-service real estate professionals while not actively participating in the transaction process beyond making the initial referral. This allows referral agents to earn income from real estate transactions without the same level of involvement and responsibility as traditional buyer or seller agents.

In some states, agents may request an active referral license in lieu of a full real estate agent license, after passing their real estate exam. In those states, if an agent requests their license to be held in referral status, referral agents cannot actively assist the client with their purchase or sale and can only refer the client. Hey...m arketing professionals who love the idea of becoming a licensed real estate agent but don't want to service clients! CaChing!

In other states, the license is the same no matter what and an agent who prefers to participate as a referral agent won't have restrictions beyond their brokerage restrictions. It will merely be a choice. Many agents who secure clients who are buying or selling outside of their (agent's) service area or state, will refer the business to a local agent. This is perfect for agents who want to service a larger market pool and for agents who want to make more money in different states without the capacity or need to get licensed in every state. You just need one license!

There are many fully licensed agents whose business model is solely focused on referring clients instead of servicing them. Think of it like being a real estate influencer who uses marketing techniques to bring in the business and connects another fully licensed agent to service the client within or outside of their expertise, focus area, or licensed state. This model is very time-efficient as the agent can focus on other goals and still get compensated (a commission) for the clients they refer to another agent. Done right, the referral agent business model can be extremely lucrative for many agents.

If showings, research, responsibility, and client management are not your thing, the referral agent business model could be a play for you!

Broker

Now here comes the confusing part. In some states, real estate agents are referred to as Brokers instead of agents. And in most states, commercial real estate agents are always called Brokers. However, titles like; Associate Broker, Broker Associate,

Broker-Salesperson or Managing Broker are generally licensed real estate agents with a broker's license without supervisory responsibilities. However, the titles and descriptions vary per state so definitely check with your real estate commission to find out how the titles line up in your state.

Does your brain hurt yet?

Now that I have your mind entangled a bit, let's make this a little easier. For the purposes of this book, when Broker is mentioned, it means, Broker of Record, Managing Broker, Broker-in-Charge, or (for some states) Supervising Broker. This type of Broker usually requires a different license and leveled-up exam or additional curriculum than required for a real estate agent. In most states, in order to become a broker, beyond the separate exam, agents need to be licensed for a specific period of time before they can become a broker. In some cases, they will also need to have worked full-time in real estate for a specific time or successfully closed a specific amount of deals. Those are the general details and because there are so many exceptions, check with your state to find out the specifics so you can determine if becoming a Broker is an option for you.

The broker is licensed to do everything a real estate agent can do with the added responsibility of supervision and oversight of agents, transactions, and operations within the brokerage they are managing. One of the Broker's primary responsibilities is to ensure that all real estate activities adhere to the relevant state and local laws and regulations governing the industry. In addition to compliance, the broker of record plays a crucial role in supervising and guiding other real estate agents and brokers affiliated with the brokerage. They provide leadership, support, and training to help agents excel in their roles. Record keeping is another essential aspect of their duties, as they maintain accurate and complete records of all transactions managed by the brokerage, ensuring full compliance with legal requirements and brokerage rules.

In the ever-evolving realm of real estate, the broker doesn't just oversee transactions but also plays a vital role in mitigating potential legal and financial risks. They're like the captain of a ship, charting a course to ensure smooth sailing. When storms of disputes or conflicts arise among agents, clients, or other parties involved in real estate transactions, it's the broker who steps up to navigate through the turbulence. They are the steady hand on the wheel, steering the ship towards resolution and keeping everyone on board safe through compliance.

Furthermore, they are responsible for overseeing agent licensing and continuing education, promoting business development efforts to expand the brokerage's client base, and providing necessary reports and updates to regulatory authorities as mandated by real estate licensing agencies. This role demands a deep understanding of real estate laws, ethical standards, and business management, as the broker is legally accountable for the actions of the agents and brokers affiliated with the brokerage. The specific duties and requirements associated with a real estate broker may vary by jurisdiction, making it essential for individuals in this role to stay well-informed about local regulations, ethics, fiduciary responsibility, and licensing criteria.

In addition, brokers may also produce business and get compensated for their real estate client's closed deals.

Flexibility

Another significant benefit of pursuing a career as a real estate agent is the unparalleled flexibility it offers. This flexibility extends to several key areas of your professional life, making it an attractive choice for individuals with diverse commitments and lifestyles. Plus, you can work from anywhere, as long as you have a phone and a laptop. In this chapter, we'll discuss many of the flexibility benefits a real estate career and business offers.

Personalized Schedule: As a real estate agent, you have the autonomy to tailor your work schedule according to your preferences as long as it aligns with the availability your ideal clients have and who are willing to pursue real estate. You can choose when to conduct property showings, client meetings, and administrative tasks. This level of control over your time will allow you to strike a harmonious balance between your work and personal life.

Work-Life Harmony: For agents with family obligations, volunteer work, or other responsibilities, real estate offers the opportunity to integrate work seamlessly into your life. You can adapt your schedule to accommodate family events, school functions, or community engagements without the constraints of a traditional 9-to-5 job or the invasive interrogating request for time off. Instead, just block the time off on your calendar, and boom!

Part-Time or Full-Time: Whether you seek to develop a full-time real estate business or wish to focus on your real estate business part-time, real estate accommodates your aspirations. Aligning your business model with SMART goals, you can invest as much or as little time as you desire, making it an ideal choice for those exploring real estate as a second career or as a supplementary income source.

Location Independence: Real estate transcends geographical boundaries. With just a cell phone, wifi, and a laptop, you can conduct business from virtually anywhere. This means you can work from home, a coffee shop, or even while traveling. The flexibility of location provides a level of freedom and adaptability that few other professions can match. Additionally, this flexibility can maximize the markets an agent has the ability to cover. Hey...ever needed to bring your kid to their 5pm game at 2pm for warm-ups? As a real estate agent, you can use the in-between time to make calls, send emails, write contracts, or create marketing elements.

Diverse Income Streams: Real estate offers opportunities for diversifying your income streams. Beyond traditional residential sales, commercial real estate, property management, or real estate investing, you can explore several niches. This diversification potential allows you to adapt your career to changing market conditions, your interests, and income goals.

The flexibility afforded by a career in real estate goes beyond setting your schedule; it permeates every aspect of your professional life. It accommodates various commitments, empowers you to work on your terms, and provides the freedom to choose your level of involvement. Whether you're embarking on a new career path or seeking supplementary income, the flexibility of real estate can help you achieve your personal and professional aspirations.

Career Autonomy

The career autonomy of a real estate agent offers unparalleled flexibility and a diverse range of business opportunities. Although various career aspects of becoming a real estate agent are referenced here, technically as an agent, you are becoming a full-out business! Within the real estate industry, there exist numerous business paths, allowing agents to tailor their professional journey to their interests and strengths. These paths encompass both residential and commercial real estate. As a real estate agent, you have the freedom to choose whether to specialize in one area or explore multiple avenues. Some agents opt to become specialists in a particular niche, while others prefer a more generalist approach. The possibilities extend far beyond simply working with buyers or sellers or solely focusing on the transaction (*as a transaction coordinator*), and with the right training and support, agents can carve out unique niches for themselves.

For instance, agents can focus exclusively on serving clients interested in Luxury or Second Homes and Vacation properties, guiding them through the complexities of these specialized markets. Alternatively, one can become an expert in navigating the intricacies of Short Sales and Foreclosures, guiding clients through challenging financial situations to find suitable solutions.

Furthermore, specialized niches such as assisting seniors in downsizing or transitioning to new living arrangements, handling real estate matters related to divorce proceedings, or managing the intricacies of Probate sales are also viable options. The real estate world is rich with diverse opportunities for those who seek to broaden their expertise and cater to specific client needs. Real estate is not your typical industry, you have endless options.

Some of the most alluring aspects of being a real estate agent can be the income potential, career autonomy, and schedule control yet the deep satisfaction that comes from assisting individuals in realizing their real estate dreams and goals is absolutely unmatched. There's a genuine sense of accomplishment in knowing that you've played a pivotal role in helping someone discover their ideal home to enhance their legacy or secure the perfect commercial space to propel their business forward. Moreover, as a real estate agent, you have the privilege of being a part of one of the most significant and exhilarating transactions in a person's life.

Multi-State Licensure

Just in case you missed it, in order to aid clients with their real estate transactions, you must hold a real estate license, in most cases in the state of your client's transaction. There are some exceptions in some states where either commercial real estate or reciprocity is concerned, but those exceptions are far and few. However, as we focused on flexibility in the last section and career autonomy in this one, I'd be remiss if I didn't mention the flexibility and independence to hold a real estate license in multiple states. Most states don't have a residence requirement which means an agent can live anywhere in the US and hold a license in any state. Servicing clients as an agent in multiple states requires the real estate agent to understand and sort out different state laws, regulations, and real estate markets. Although this might be a challenge for some, it's the perfect fit for many agents.

There are many reasons an agent might decide to get licensed in another state or country for that matter but for this book, we'll stick with states in the US. Before you make that decision, be sure that it aligns with your SMART strategic business goals. To give you some ideas, some of the popular reasons I've come across are below.

- The agent lives near the border of a state with a thriving real estate market.

- The agent lives in one state but frequents another to visit family/friends, vacation, do business, or where they own other real estate.

- The agent lives in one state but previously lived in another where they also understand the market.

- The agent lives in a state where they find many of their seller clients are migrating to another state for convenience, weather, price, or even work. For example, agents that focus on seniors as a niche might notice that their clients are selling their homes and downsizing, purchasing smaller homes in warmer states after they retire.

- The agent is affiliated with a brokerage that has a team in their additional state of desired licensure.
- The agent plans to move to the state where they hold their additional state licensure.

There are several other reasons an agent might take this route. However, make sure your goal to license in additional states is SMART. Keep in mind that just as you can take the steps to license in multiple states, there are other ways to service clients in other states. You can also opt to build relationships with agents in other states to whom you refer your clients who are relocating. The process of referring clients to agents you trust could also serve as a lucrative revenue stream minus the weight of licensure and with a little less work.

- Depending on the states for licensure (in addition to other pre-requisites), agents may be required to take a full real estate exam, just the state exam, or in states with full reciprocity, no exam at all. Do your research and take one state on at a time.

My Story: I am licensed in multiple states with strategic intention. For one, I own the brokerage I'm licensed with and although multi-state licensure is not a requirement for me, I want to ensure that I am also able to supply the information our agents need to thrive and service their clients and in a pinch, I can jump in and assist agents if needed. Secondly, multi-state licensure is a part of my company's strategic business goals to serve clients in specific states. Other reasons connect to our capacity and the dreams we have for the brokerage we have built. Some of the other reasons why we decided the strategic business goals for our company would include multiple states are included in the popular reasons many agents decide to license in multiple states previously.

Niche Market Descriptions

There are several niche opportunities available in real estate and way too many to list here. However, here are a few just to get your juices flowing.

55+ Active Adult Communities: Specialize in assisting older adults looking to downsize or transition to active adult communities tailored to their needs and preferences.

Commercial Leasing or Sales: Focus on commercial real estate, either leasing or sales, including office spaces, retail spaces, warehouses, and more, assisting businesses in finding suitable locations to thrive.

Eco-Friendly and Sustainable Homes: Focus on helping clients find environmentally friendly and energy-efficient homes that align with their commitment to sustainability.

First-Time Homebuyer: Specialize in assisting individuals or families purchasing their first home, guiding them through the entire home buying process, and providing essential support for a smooth experience.

Investor: Focus on working with real estate investors looking to build wealth through property acquisitions, analyzing investment opportunities, and providing expert advice on potential returns.

Side Note: Investors are often repeat buyers and sellers. And if your investor client fixes and flips properties...you could represent the same client on several properties twice (buy and sell) each time! Also, if you are an investor with a real estate license...you could potentially double and triple your bag with this niche!

Luxury: Cater to high-end clientele seeking luxury properties, showcasing exceptional properties, and offering personalized service to meet the unique needs and desires of affluent buyers and sellers.

Military Relocation Specialist: Support military personnel and their families with their unique relocation needs, considering factors like proximity to bases and amenities.

Property Management: Specialize in managing properties on behalf of owners, overseeing leasing, maintenance, rent collection, and tenant relationships to ensure optimal returns for residential or commercial property owners.

Short Sales and Foreclosure: Focus on assisting clients with distressed properties, particularly for short sales (properties sold for less than the mortgage balance) and foreclosures (properties seized by lenders due to non-payment). These specialists navigate the complex processes involved in these types of transactions, helping clients negotiate with lenders, mitigate financial challenges, and find opportunities for potential investment or homeownership at reduced prices. *Requires a special license or permit in some states.*

Transaction Coordinator: Offer transaction coordination services, helping other agents and clients navigate the complexities of real estate transactions, ensuring a smooth and organized process from contract to closing.

Vacation or Second Home Specialist: Specialize in vacation properties, helping clients find the perfect vacation home or investment property in sought-after destinations, such as beachfront, mountain resorts, or serene getaways.

Most of the niches mentioned here do not require a separate license from what you'll get from your state when you become a real estate agent, but many have optional designations and certifications. If you really want to be at the top of your game and recognized as an expert, check the National Association of Realtors for certification courses connected to your niche after becoming licensed. Embracing your passion and matching it with a niche that aligns with your interests and strengths is an excellent way to narrow your focus and set the stage for a fulfilling career that will set your real estate business apart from other agents.

However, no matter what your approach is, *niche or not*, recognizing and embracing your love for real estate will be your driving force toward a fulfilling career. Let your passion guide you as you position yourself to leap forward and level up while embarking on a career and building a business with opportunities in the dynamic realm of real estate.

To Sum It Up: The business-building career of a real estate agent offers unmatched autonomy, allowing professionals to choose from a wide array of career paths and specialization options, set their schedules, and control their income. With the right training and determination, agents can excel in their chosen niches, providing valuable services to clients and building a fulfilling and prosperous business and career in the dynamic world of real estate.

Chapter Three

School Days

Selecting the Optimal Real Estate Licensing Test Prep School or Online Course

Embarking on the journey to become a licensed real estate agent is an exciting endeavor, but it all begins with a critical step: choosing the right test prep school or online course. The significance of this choice cannot be overstated, as it lays the foundation for your education and training, ultimately determining your readiness to successfully pass the official licensure exam. In this chapter, we will explore in depth the essential aspects of finding the ideal educational pathway.

Research and Comparison

Start your quest by conducting thorough research on different schools. Compare between test prep schools and online courses for the specific state you plan to attain your real estate license. This initial step will enable you to discern the best options available in the market. Your options may also include in-person vs. online as well as various course lengths, paces, and schedules. To organize your thoughts, create a spreadsheet with headers and a rating system to help with selection.

Reviews: Seek out institutions with a proven track record of high success rates among their students. This is a good indicator of the quality of education they provide. Additionally, consider reading reviews and testimonials from previous students to gain insights into their experiences and outcomes.

Success Rate and State vs. National Exam Pass Rate: It's crucial to differentiate between the success rate of the school's internal assessments and the pass rate of students on the official state and national exams. Many states require students to pass a school exam before they can proceed to take the official licensure exams. Thus, while a school's success rate is important, researching the percentage of students who successfully pass the official state and national exams is a strong key indicator of your likelihood of obtaining licensure.

Also, if you are already licensed in certain professions like as an attorney for example, some states may offer a waiver for you to skip the class, all or a portion of the exam. Veterans may also receive perks in some states when it comes to fees, school or exams as certain levels. Check your state criteria to confirm your eligibility for waivers or other opportunities.

Cost and Time Considerations

While the value of a high-quality education cannot be overstated, it's equally vital to align your choice with your financial resources, your schedule, and other needs. To make an informed decision, you should assess the financial aspects of each program thoroughly, taking into account tuition fees, required materials, and any supplementary expenses that may arise during your course of study. Additionally, keep a keen eye out for any discounts, financial aid, or scholarship opportunities that could alleviate the cost burden.

Moreover, it's worth noting that many educational institutions offer a range of pace options to accommodate diverse student needs. These options can vary from accelerated programs to full-time and part-time schedules. When making your selection, it's essential to choose a pace that not only suits your lifestyle but also flows seamlessly with your existing commitments. It is possible that you may need to adjust your schedule to accommodate the course but consider your current schedule with a realistic lens and analyze the amount of available time you can dedicate to the course. This includes factoring in the time needed for completing homework assignments and thoroughly comprehending the study materials. By aligning your course pace with your schedule realistically, you can ensure a smoother and more manageable educational journey.

Food for Thought: While course lengths vary, all the material required for the exam gets covered regardless of course length with a reputable and accredited school or course provider. *For example, a 9-day consecutive real estate course may be great for your schedule if you have a week and a half to squeeze in the course. In contrast, a 2-month course meeting weekly may give you more time to think through challenges understanding the material, to ask the instructors questions and study between classes to retain the material.*

Some states allow self-paced courses, which provide prospective agents months to unlimited time to revisit all topic areas to ensure material retention. However, self-paced courses usually are absent of a live tangible instructor, so know your learning style and select the best course for your style.

No matter what time sequence you select, enroll in a course over a period that gives you enough time (*emphasis on enough time*) to retain the information necessary for the school test and National and State exams. Many in-person schools offer courses over varied periods of time. The Real Estate exam includes robust information on various real estate topics. Some topics, rules, or regulations may seem foreign, while others are similar but different between state and federal, so planning enough time to digest the information is absolutely essential.

More of My Story: My schedule is usually full and I find myself achieving goals and leveling up with a wealth of intrinsic strategic pushes and squeezing massive things into small buckets of time. I am also a strategic planner, with decent information retention and good study habits habits so I initially created an unrelenting aggressive course schedule and study goal. It was simple, take a consecutive nine-day virtual course with a live instructor and sit for the exam a few days later. Ha! Nice try, that did NOT happen. Goals are important, but make sure they follow the SMART system, with an emphasis on Reasonable, when it comes to planning out your study and test-taking plans.

Location, Location, Location

The decision between an in-person test prep school with a physical location and the convenience of an online course is a pivotal one. This choice should be guided by various factors, all of which contribute to the effectiveness and ease of your learning experience.

- **Geographic Considerations**: Begin by evaluating your geographic location. If you live in close proximity to a physical test prep school and prefer face-to-face interaction with instructors and fellow students, an in-person option may be appealing. However, if you reside in a remote area or have limited access to physical institutions, an online course offers the advantage of accessibility, allowing you to participate in your chosen program from virtually anywhere.

- **Schedule Flexibility**: Take into account your schedule constraints, which can significantly influence your decision. In-person classes often adhere to fixed schedules, which may or may not align with your availability. Conversely, online courses typically offer greater flexibility, allowing you to set your own study pace and tailor your learning to fit within your existing commitments.

- **Personal Learning Preferences**: Reflect on your personal learning style and preferences. Some individuals thrive in a classroom environment, benefiting from in-person interactions and structured routines. Others find that the self-paced or virtual online courses better suit their learning needs, providing the autonomy to delve deeper into specific topics or revisit materials as needed.

Note: *There is a difference between self-paced and virtual online courses. A self-paced course will give you the autonomy to study and work through the course at your own pace. Whereas a virtual online course is often instructor-led and will give you the opportunity to take the course in your preferred comfort yet at a designated time with a dedicated instructor, who might require screens on and class participation.*

- **Technological Comfort**: Consider your comfort level with technology. Online courses require a degree of digital literacy, as you'll be engaging with course materials and resources through digital platforms. Ensure that you have the necessary access to a reliable internet connection and the requisite devices to support your online learning.
- **Support Systems**: Evaluate the support systems available to you. In-person institutions often offer on-site assistance, while online courses typically provide online forums, email support, and virtual office hours. Choose the format that aligns with your preferred mode of seeking help and guidance.

To Sum It Up, the choice between in-person and online test prep options is multifaceted and should be based on your individual circumstances and preferences. Assess your location, scheduling needs, learning style, technological readiness, and the level of support you require to make an informed decision that sets you up for a successful journey toward real estate licensure.

Curriculum and Resources

Delve into the details of the curriculum offered by each school or course. Ensure that it comprehensively covers the topics and materials required for success on the licensure exam. Additionally, inquire about the availability of supplementary resources, such as practice exams and study guides.

Accreditation and Licensing

Confirm that the institution you choose is accredited by relevant authorities and recognized by your chosen state of licensure real estate licensing commission or board. This ensures that your education meets the necessary standards for licensure in that state. In some states, this won't be necessary, but it's good to know in the event your state requires accreditation.

Student Support and Interaction

Assess the level of student support provided by the institution. This includes access to instructors, tutors, or support staff who can address your questions and concerns. Interaction with fellow students can also enhance your learning experience. While student engagement can be helpful, be sure to understand your learning style because some students absorb material better on their own without interaction while it may boost learning for others.

Study Methods and Tools

Explore the teaching methods and tools employed by the test prep school or online course. Modern, interactive learning platforms and a variety of instructional resources can contribute to a more effective learning process. Confirm how long you'll have access to study aids post-course completion.

My Story: While the school I attended for the first state I became licensed did not offer study aids beyond the purchased text that came with the course, I took advantage of the opportunity to create a study group since I was part of a live virtual class. This helped me sort out information that didn't initially make sense and learn different mnemonic devices others were using to help them connect and retain the information. Additionally, I utilized a few different online exam prep sites after I completed the school exam in preparation for the official national and state licensing exam.

Failure, In The Worst Case Scenario

Failure and the "F" bomb could look like twins. However, if you don't succeed the first time, can you try again? Many states require that you pass a school exam before you sit for the state and national exams. Confirm what happens if you fail the school exam and how many times you are allowed to retake the school exam before you are either booted out or have to retake the course. Inquire about any additional costs in the event of failure. Keep in mind, that passing the real estate exam is essential to become a licensed real estate agent. However, the need to try again won't determine your success or lack thereof as an agent unless you allow failure to defeat you.

To Sum It Up: Your journey to becoming a licensed real estate agent commences with selecting the right test prep school, study tools or online course. Thorough research, consideration of success rates and reviews, cost assessment, and attention to factors like location and flexibility are essential elements in making an informed decision. By choosing wisely, you lay the groundwork for a successful and rewarding career in real estate.

Chapter Four

Real Estate School Exam

Effective Study Strategies and Prep

Some prospective agents, for better or for worse get to skip this step. The school exam is only mandatory for prospective agents seeking licensure in states that require a real estate licensing course and pass it before attempting the state exam. Some states allow prospective agents to bypass this step (real estate course and school exam) and instead go straight to the state exam if they served in the armed forces, are actively licensed in other states, or hold a college degree with a focus on real estate. Check with your real estate commission to confirm if passing a real estate course with an accredited real estate school is a pre-requisite.

Once you've enrolled in a test prep school or online course, the next step is to prepare for the school exam. This examination serves as a foundational assessment of your grasp of the fundamental principles and practices within the realm of real estate. To succeed, it's paramount to approach your studies with diligence and strategic planning. In this chapter, we will discuss the comprehensive strategies to enhance your preparation for the school exam.

Structure and Routine Study Schedule

Begin by crafting a well-structured study schedule tailored to your pace and commitments. Consistency is key, so allocate dedicated time each day or week to review the material. Breaking down the extensive content into manageable portions of time ensures thorough coverage. Adjust your focus or intensity of study of specific areas as you begin to retain and comprehend the material.

Pro Study Tip: Organize your study time on a digital calendar and set reminders just like you would for a business meeting so you don't miss this very important part of your day.

Topic-Centric Learning

Initially, focus your attention on one topic at a time. This approach allows for deeper comprehension and retention of information. As you master each subject, you'll build a strong foundation for tackling the comprehensive exam. However, remember that the exams are robust so continue to review information that you've studied and mastered previously to aid in your retention.

Pro Study Tip: As you move on to new topics, include time in your calendar to revisit previously mastered topics regularly.

Power of Study Aids

Elevate your learning journey by making effective use of diverse study aids. These resources can significantly enhance your retention and understanding retention of crucial real estate concepts and terminologies. The more questions you are able to answer in different formats will dually increase your comprehension and retention.

- **Flashcards for Reinforcement:** Flashcards are a fantastic tool to reinforce key concepts and terminologies. By condensing the information into bite-sized chunks and quizzing yourself regularly, you can ingrain essential knowledge into your memory more effectively.
- **Practice Exams for Self-Assessment:** Practice exams serve as invaluable instruments for evaluating your progress and identifying areas that demand further attention. Simulating the exam environment helps you adapt to the test format and refine your time management skills.

Pro Study Tip: Give yourself a break from the textbook and add study questions and the answers you are experiencing difficulty with into an online self-study quiz tool, digital flash-cards, or use an online testing software that allows you to focus on specific sections of the exam.
Include lots of questions asked in different formats in your study plan. The official test requires you to not only remember the information but also comprehend it so make sure you quiz yourself in different ways to maximize comprehension and increase your confidence.

- **Collaborative Learning in Study Groups:** Consider joining study groups as they offer a dynamic and collaborative learning environment. Engaging with fellow learners allows you to exchange insights, discuss challenging topics, and clarify doubts. Peer interactions can provide fresh perspectives and reinforce your understanding of the material.

- **Sensory Engagement:** It's essential to recognize the significance of sensory engagement in the learning process. Combining sensory experiences—such as reading aloud, writing, and hearing—can enhance the memorization of material. Reading aloud reinforces auditory memory while writing information down reinforces visual and kinesthetic memory. By incorporating these sensory approaches alongside your chosen study aids, you create a multi-dimensional learning experience that strengthens your grasp of real estate concepts, setting the stage for your success in the school exam and beyond.

- **Acronyms aka Brain Cheats:** There is an abundance of material to comprehend and memorize for the real estate exam which can feel overwhelming. However, there are what I call brain cheats you can use such as mnemonic devices and acronyms, phrases, rhymes, songs, etc. to help you remember the material or at least some of it. You'll find quite a few in your text during study like:

- **OLD CAR** which is an acronym frequently used to remember a real estate agent's fiduciary (obedience, loyalty, disclosure, confidentiality, reasonable care/diligence) not the age of the car they drive.

- **PITI** (principle, interest, taxes, and insurance) which relates to mortgages not to be confused with...PITT

- **PITT** (possession, interest, time, and title) which relates to joint tenancy. Embrace all of the mnemonic devices and if you develop others that are easier for you to remember, use them.

- There are 43,560 feet in an acre which is commonly remembered by using **4 old people driving 35 miles** per hour on a 60-mile-per-hour highway or **7/11** because 4+3=7 and 5+6=11.

My Story: During my study, for some reason, I had a terrible time remembering the difference between Freddie Mac (FHLMC) and Ginnie Mae (GNMA), both have much longer names, by the way. Anyway, I've found (for the exam) that remembering one unique term or fact about a topic will help with the process of elimination when both similar topics or the other are presented.

At some point, (just for the exam) to untangle that information, I linked Ginnie Mae to Jenny from the block (aka J-LO). Stay with me, because I passed several real estate exams on the first try. I associated the idea that (in short) part of Ginnie Mae's purpose guarantees housing programs for low-moderate income borrowers with the idea that Jenny (J-Lo) from the block was from the Bronx which has some low-moderate income purchasers. I additionally connected Ginnie Mae pass-through securities with the fact that when I visit the Bronx, I am only passing through since I don't live there. Sure, many cities around the world have low-income purchasers but there is only one Jenny (J-Lo) from the Bronx and only one Ginnie Mae. That wild way of connecting information in my head ended up being the right dose of unique crazy to help me sort out the difference between Ginnie and Freddie and make the information stick for the exam.

Find your own mnemonic devices aka brain cheats to get information to stick in your brain. Songs, rhymes, phrases, celebrities, food, cars, cities...you name it, are all options. **If you didn't scan this QR Code before, this is your moment! Scan it now to get a list of over 30 brain cheats to help study for the exam.**

Interactive Learning Resources

Explore interactive learning resources offered by your test prep school or online course, and consider the length of access to these valuable materials even after the course concludes *(if offered by the test prep school)*. These resources are designed to enhance your mastery and understanding of complex real estate topics.

- **Multimedia Enrichment:** Investigate if the program integrates multimedia elements into its curriculum. These can include videos, animations, and audio components that bring concepts to life. Multimedia not only adds depth to your learning experience but also caters to various learning styles and attention spans, making it easier to grasp and retain information.

- **Simulations for Practical Application:** Look for the inclusion of simulations that allow you to apply theoretical knowledge to practical scenarios. Simulations provide a hands-on approach to learning and help you develop problem-solving skills relevant to real estate transactions.
- **Interactive Exercises:** Assess the availability of interactive exercises that engage you actively with the course material. These exercises may involve quizzes, case studies, students in your cohort or interactive assessments that reinforce your understanding and offer immediate feedback to track your progress.

Additionally, consider using a test prep course or simulator specifically designed for the state and national exam to ensure you are adequately prepared for the test layout and question structure. Your coursework may have done an excellent job covering this, but remember that not all schools and courses are built the same.

Pro Study Tip: Inquire about the duration of your access to these interactive resources post-course completion. Retaining access beyond the course's conclusion can be immensely beneficial, as it allows you to revisit materials for reinforcement or reference as you embark on your real estate career.

Incorporating these interactive learning resources into your study routine fosters a more comprehensive and engaging learning experience, equipping you with the skills and knowledge needed to excel in the real estate industry.

Seek Clarification

It's paramount not to hesitate when you encounter challenges or have questions during your course, especially if your program offers instructional support. If your course provides access to instructors or tutors, take full advantage of this valuable resource. In the event your course does not offer such support, consider reaching out to a trusted real estate agent coach, trainer, mentor, or an experienced real estate broker within your network. Clarifying doubts promptly with someone who thoroughly understands the material can prevent misconceptions from taking root and hindering your progress.

Here's why seeking clarification is of utmost importance:

- **Prevents Misconceptions**: Promptly clarifying doubts with an expert who thoroughly understands the material is essential in preventing misconceptions from taking root. Misunderstandings can hinder your progress and lead to inaccuracies in your understanding of critical real estate concepts.

- **Clarify Complex Topics:** Real estate can involve intricate and nuanced concepts that may be challenging to grasp initially. Reaching out for clarification allows you to gain deeper insights into these complex topics, ensuring a more robust understanding.

- **Customize Guidance:** Instructors, tutors, coaches, and experienced brokers can provide tailored guidance based on your specific questions and needs. This personalized assistance can expedite your learning process and help you overcome hurdles more effectively.

- **Enhance Confidence:** Having a reliable source for clarification boosts your confidence in your knowledge and abilities. It ensures that you enter the school exam well-prepared, reducing anxiety and increasing your chances of success.
- **Building Professional Relationships:** Establishing connections with instructors, coaches, trainers, or experienced brokers can also serve as the foundation for valuable professional relationships in the real estate industry. These connections may offer ongoing guidance and support as you embark on your career.

Pro Study Tip: It's worth noting that, depending on your state's rules and regulations, you will need to interview real estate brokerages to affiliate with after your exam. In addition to seeking clarification on course-related questions, consider reaching out to a brokerage you may be interested in joining. *See Chapter 5, Finding the Right Brokerage, and use it as a proactive approach to dually connecting with real estate brokerages and learning about its benefits can help you now and later.*

Seeking clarification during your educational journey is crucial, but it's equally vital to think long-term. Proactively reaching out to potential brokerages serves a dual purpose: it not only helps resolve any uncertainties you may have but also empowers you to make well-informed decisions about your future in the real estate industry. Whether you're seeking answers from your course instructors, trusted mentors, or seasoned professionals, timely clarification not only strengthens your comprehension but also positions you for success in the dynamic world of real estate. Never underestimate the significance of seeking clarification when you encounter challenges or have questions during your real estate education.

Self-Assessment

Regular self-assessment is a fundamental practice on your journey to becoming a licensed real estate agent. It serves as a crucial mechanism for tracking your progress, identifying strengths, and pinpointing areas that demand additional focus. By incorporating this self-assessment into your study routine, you can effectively fine-tune your preparation for the school exam.

To begin with, regularly challenging yourself with quizzes and self-assessment tools is essential. These resources not only evaluate your grasp of the material but also mimic the format of the exam itself. This helps you acclimate to the test's structure, timing, and question types, reducing potential test-day anxiety.

Actively engage your senses during the learning process. Take advantage of online self-assessment resources that also allow self-inputting of information which will aid memory utilizing sensory during input. Regularly challenge yourself with quizzes and leverage online self-assessment resources that enable you to input information, thereby enhancing memory retention through sensory input.

Furthermore, self-assessment aids in pinpointing your strong points and areas that require improvement. By recognizing where you excel, you can allocate your study time more efficiently, concentrating on topics that demand greater attention. This targeted approach enhances the overall effectiveness of your preparation, ensuring that you enter the exam with a well-rounded understanding of the subject matter.

Self-assessment also promotes a sense of accountability and ownership over your learning journey. It empowers you to take charge of your progress, set achievable milestones, and make necessary adjustments to your study plan. This proactive approach is instrumental in achieving your goal of passing the school exam with confidence.

To Sum It Up: self-assessment is not merely an optional practice but an indispensable tool in your arsenal as you prepare for the school exam. Regularly challenging yourself, identifying areas for improvement, and adjusting your study strategy accordingly all contribute to a more robust and effective preparation, ultimately positioning you for success in your pursuit of a real estate career.

Real-World Application

Bridging the gap between theoretical knowledge and practical application is a pivotal aspect of your real estate education. By delving into how concepts manifest in real-life scenarios, you can not only deepen your understanding but also fortify your memory retention. The practicality of real estate comes to life through numerous examples, highlighting the relevance of this approach:

- **Contracts and Disclosures:** Practical application in contracts and disclosures involves drafting legally sound agreements and ensuring that all relevant information is accurately disclosed to parties involved in a transaction. This hands-on experience is vital for safeguarding the interests of your clients and adhering to legal requirements.

- **Agency and Ethics:** Applying theoretical concepts of agency and ethics in real-world scenarios is essential for maintaining high ethical standards and fostering trust with clients. Real-world situations may involve initializing and explaining the different types of agency, navigating potential conflicts of interest, maintaining confidentiality, and upholding fiduciary duties.

- **Legal Compliance:** Real estate transactions involve complex legal considerations that require strict adherence to regulations. Practical application may involve conducting due diligence on property titles, ensuring compliance with local zoning laws, and addressing legal challenges that may arise during a transaction.

To bridge the theory-practice gap effectively, leveraging relationships with experienced real estate brokers, coaches, mentors, and trainers is invaluable. Their guidance and real-world insights offer you a richer perspective on how to apply your knowledge to actual real estate transactions, ensuring you are well-prepared for a successful career in the field.

Manage Stress and Maintain Health

Managing stress and maintaining your overall health are essential components of your journey to becoming a licensed real estate agent. Preparing for a rigorous exam demands not only mental acuity but also physical well-being. To ensure you're performing at your best, prioritize self-care as an integral part of your study routine which includes maintaining a balanced lifestyle with proper nutrition, exercise, and sufficient rest.

First and foremost, maintaining a balanced lifestyle is paramount. This includes understanding what you need to thrive while ensuring the needs in your regular life before any exam, are met. Additionally, adhering to a nutrient-rich diet that fuels your body and brain with the energy needed for focused learning. Regular exercise is equally vital; physical activity not only promotes physical fitness but also boosts cognitive function and helps alleviate stress.

Sufficient rest is another critical element of self-care. Adequate sleep is when your brain consolidates information learned throughout the day, enhancing memory retention. It also allows your body to rejuvenate, ensuring you wake up refreshed and ready to tackle your study goals.

Effective stress management techniques are invaluable during your exam preparation. High-stress levels can impair cognitive abilities and hinder your ability to absorb and retain information. Engage in activities that help with relaxation and stress reduction, such as deep breathing exercises, and meditation. or mindfulness practices.

To Sum It Up: your journey toward real estate licensure is not solely about acquiring knowledge but also about maintaining a healthy body and mind. Prioritizing self-care through nutrition, exercise, rest, and stress management will not only enhance your cognitive abilities but also contribute to your overall well-being, ensuring you're well-prepared to excel in your school exam and your future real estate career.

Review and Revise

Periodically reviewing and revising previously studied material is a fundamental strategy that can significantly boost your preparedness for the real estate school exam. Rather than simply focusing on acquiring new knowledge, this practice involves revisiting and consolidating what you've already learned.

By regularly reviewing past material, you reinforce your memory, ensuring that critical concepts remain readily accessible in your mind. This not only helps prevent forgetting but also solidifies your understanding of key topics. Over time, this disciplined approach builds a robust foundation of knowledge that you can rely on during the exam.

Moreover, review and revision allow you to identify any gaps in your comprehension and address them proactively. It's an opportunity to revisit challenging areas, clarify doubts, and gain a deeper insight into complex subjects. As you revisit the material, consider different perspectives and practical applications to enrich your understanding further.

Incorporating review and revision into your study routine is akin to constructing a sturdy mental framework upon which you can build your real estate knowledge. It's a practice that not only ensures you retain what you've learned but also reinforces your overall grasp of the subject matter, ultimately bolstering your confidence and readiness for exam day.

Simulate Exam Conditions

As the date of your real estate school exam draws near, it's imperative to take your exam preparation a step further by simulating exam conditions during your practice tests. This deliberate approach serves several vital purposes including reducing anxiety and improving your performance for the actual examination.

Additionally, simulating exam conditions provides an opportunity to acquaint yourself with the time constraints that the real exam imposes. By timing yourself during practice tests, you gain a realistic sense of the pace at which you need to work through questions and allocate time to each section. This experience is invaluable in managing your time effectively during the actual exam, preventing rushed decisions, and ensuring you can complete all sections within the allotted time frame.

Furthermore, the familiarity you develop with the exam environment through simulation is instrumental in reducing anxiety. Entering the exam room with a sense of déjà vu can significantly calm nerves and boost confidence. You'll feel more at ease, as the surroundings and conditions will feel less intimidating and more routine, ultimately enhancing your performance.

Simulating exam conditions is not merely about testing your knowledge but also about honing your test-taking skills. It's an opportunity to fine-tune your strategies for approaching different question types and managing your time wisely. Through consistent practice in a simulated exam setting, you'll be better equipped to navigate the challenges and complexities of the real estate school exam, ensuring that you enter the testing center with confidence and a well-prepared mindset.

My Story: During one of my in-person state exams, I wore a sweater because I like to layer. It was comfortable yet almost chilly in the registration room so I thought...good thing I have this sweater on. Well, that changed as soon as I walked into the official testing room. Upon arriving at my exam seat, I noticed how uncomfortably warm it was (no not nerves, actually heat) and I knew I wouldn't last with the sweater on. Before I sat down at the computer, I immediately removed the sweater and placed it on the back of my chair. Within seconds, very much like a SWAT team, the exam representatives (through the glass window) gave me all types of waves and faces and because I didn't get the hint (who me?), they came running into the room demanding that I put the sweater back on or hang it in the waiting room. Stunned, I ran out and hung it in the waiting room because there was no way I was going to be able to test in the heat of the desert that was swarming in the room.

When simulating the exam conditions, it's best to consider the little things like wearing layers. Minimally, you can remove a layer before the exam if the testing room is too hot.

To Sum It Up, effective preparation for the real estate school exam necessitates a thorough and strategic approach. This includes establishing a well-structured study schedule, concentrating on specific subjects, leveraging study aids and interactive resources, seeking timely clarification, and prioritizing your physical and mental well-being. These strategies collectively equip you with the tools to excel in your school exam, laying a strong foundation for your future success in the real estate industry.

Chapter Five

State and National Exam

Effective Study Strategies and Prep

After passing the school exam, celebrate! Just be aware that you are not done yet. The next hurdle is the state and national exams. This exam (depending on your state) could be offered in one or two parts. Regardless, it covers federal, local, and state-specific laws and regulations and agency practices related to real estate, so it's important to study the material thoroughly.

Consider using the same study tactics as you did for the school exam, but also make sure to review the material regularly. Create a plan to schedule and pass your exam well within the state testing requirements to eliminate the need to retake the course *(if a course is required)*. But also to ensure you have time to try again if you don't succeed the first time. Some states give you one year from the time you started your exam prep course, but DO NOT WAIT THAT LONG! Emphasis on the all caps!

Kick up your study habits for full comprehension: It's important to recognize that the rigor of your coursework in your chosen real estate school or online program may vary, and as a result, the state and national exam could potentially pose a greater level of difficulty than the school exam. Therefore, it's crucial to remain adaptable and prepared to elevate your study habits as needed. This means being open to the possibility of encountering more complex material and adjusting your approach to match the demands of the official exams. While the school exam serves as a foundation, the official state and national exams often require a deeper level of understanding of real estate principles and practices. To meet this challenge effectively, consider allocating additional time and resources to enhance your knowledge, practice problem-solving, and gain a thorough grasp of the intricacies involved. By maintaining a proactive and adaptable mindset, you can position yourself for success in both the school exam and the more rigorous state and national exams, ensuring that you meet the requirements for real estate licensure with confidence and competence.

Once you've successfully passed your school exam, it's imperative to transition seamlessly into preparing for your state and national exams. While it's essential to take the necessary time to study and consolidate your knowledge, it's equally crucial not to delay scheduling your state and national exams. The reason for this urgency is simple: you want to capitalize on the momentum and familiarity you've gained with the study material and practice testing techniques while they are still fresh in your mind.

Pro Study Tip: Continue a regular study schedule until you pass the state and national exams.

By promptly scheduling your state and national exams, you maintain the continuity of your learning process. This proactive approach ensures that you stay engaged with the subject matter and retain the valuable insights and strategies you've developed during your school exam preparation. It also minimizes the risk of forgetting key concepts or losing the proficiency you've gained in tackling exam questions.

Furthermore, scheduling your state and national exams sooner rather than later offers several advantages. It sets a clear and tangible goal, motivating you to stay committed to your study regimen. It also allows you to allocate your study time more efficiently, focusing on the areas that require additional attention and reducing unnecessary stress as your exam date approaches.

There's an additional compelling reason to schedule your state and national exam promptly after successfully clearing your school exam – the availability of testing dates. Testing centers tend to fill up quickly, and popular exam dates may become scarce if you delay your scheduling. By taking proactive steps and securing your exam date sooner, you increase the likelihood of obtaining your preferred testing date and reduce your study time.

Moreover, scheduling early provides you with a sense of certainty and structure in your exam preparation timeline. It allows you to set a clear target date to work toward, which can be a motivating factor as you continue to study and refine your knowledge and skills.

Pro Exam Tip: Promptly schedule your state and national exams shortly after you pass the school exam. If you are taking a self-paced exam schedule the exam when you reach or exceed 10-15 points higher in each category than what is required to pass the state and national exam. This is of course if you are scoring less than an 85%. Even though you may need a lower score depending on your state, you want to score as high as possible on your practice exam because the official exam will most likely offer a higher level of difficulty.

By scheduling your exam soon after you complete your course you not only secure your preferred testing date but also gain a sense of clarity and motivation in your exam preparation efforts.

More of My Exam Story: It was going to be a succinct, short, and sweet "one and done" for me. I was very vocal about my determination to pass the real estate exam on my very first attempt. I had absolutely no intention of sitting for the real estate exam more than once. However, my journey didn't unfold exactly as planned.

The day I was scheduled to take my exam as planned (*I'm pretty sure God was laughing at my plan when I put it together*) there was a technical glitch before I could start testing. It took over three hours to correct which included testing screens with the exam team online, to thinking it was resolved to find out it wasn't repeatedly. The lack of patience and full-on irritation I developed through that process forced me to reschedule. I was no longer in the fully mentally prepared headspace that I was when I woke up that morning. Due to my upcoming schedule, it would be a while before I could sit for this exam, so my initial plans to take a consecutive 9-day course and test a few days later would not happen and the quest to find time would begin.

In not the wisest way, I paused my study after the technical debacle. Then when I found a date to retest that worked with my schedule, I felt like I didn't remember enough and needed to re-study. Although a longer route, it all worked out in the end. I did pass the exam on my first try and...I also had additional first-try passes in every other state I attempted to get licensed.

Gluten for punishment or strategic goals...you tell me!

The moral of the story, test immediately after your school exam or online study is complete and continue your study regime until you successfully pass!

Celebrate

Immediately after you've passed your state and national exams, celebrate! And...give yourself a well-deserved break from your intensive study routine. With licensure in sight, you can temporarily retire your study aids, knowing that you've achieved a significant milestone in your real estate journey. This respite allows you to recharge and focus on other aspects of your career preparation, such as networking, interview preparations, or exploring potential brokerage affiliations.

What Other Agents Say

Many agents say that the real estate exam study process is definitely not for the weak, nor is passing it on your first try. The challenge encompasses the volumes of material necessary for retention and comprehension combined with the test format. Yet with the right preparation (and time), you can fly through the exam and pass it on your very first try.

Facts

And...honestly, if you don't succeed on your first try, reset, restudy, and try again. The goal is to get licensed and as long as you get there, who cares how many attempts it took? The course for the exam is going to teach a lot, but it won't teach you how to win in the real estate business. Therefore, if you happen to fail, don't let that failure stop you from getting back on the horse again--try again.

The number of attempts it takes to pass the exam is not indicative of how you'll perform as an agent in the real estate business. Basically, you need the license to operate as an agent or broker in the business. Much of the information you need to know for the licensing exam will help you learn how to keep your license. After you've passed the test and you're in the business depending on your current proficiency, you may want to seek out additional coursework on topics that directly relate to your niche, marketing, compliance, systems, lead generation, and more.

To Sum It Up: while it's crucial to dedicate sufficient time to study for your state and national exams, it's equally important to seize the opportunity to schedule these exams promptly (near your successful course completion date). By doing so, you maximize your chances of success by capitalizing on your current knowledge and maintaining your exam readiness. This proactive approach not only keeps you on track but also positions you for a smoother and more confident transition from school exams to official licensure exams. Additionally, the sooner you successfully pass the state and national exams, you can take a breather from your rigorous study routine and shift your focus toward other critical aspects of launching your real estate career.

Another BONUS! If you didn't scan the QR Code in one of the prior chapters, now is your moment! Scan for FREE access to the bonuses offered prior and..my favorite test prep resources!

Chapter Six

Navigating Pre-Licensing Laws for Real Estate Agents

Before embarking on the journey to becoming a licensed real estate agent, it's important to understand the pre-licensing requirements, laws, rules, and or regulations that govern the real estate in your specific state. These laws vary by state but generally include requirements such as completing a certain number of education hours, passing a background check, and passing the state exam. Make sure you are familiar with these laws and requirements to ensure a smooth licensing process. Visiting the website of the state of your chosen licensure's Real Estate Commission is a good place to start. Additionally, consider seeking guidance from a knowledgeable mentor or real estate professional to help guide you through the process.

Pro Tip: Reach out to a real estate brokerage you are interested in joining or your preferred real estate school and request any information they have regarding pre-licensure.

Understanding State-Specific Requirements

One of the primary aspects of pre-licensing laws involves comprehending the specific requirements set forth by your state's Real Estate Commission. These requirements typically encompass several key elements, including the number of education hours you must complete, the need to pass a background check (and in some states credit check), and the successful completion of the state exam. Familiarizing yourself with these state-specific requirements is the first step in ensuring a seamless journey toward real estate licensure.

Education Hour Requirements

Many states mandate a specific number of education hours as part of their pre-licensing requirements. These hours are typically completed through accredited real estate schools or online courses. The curriculum covers essential topics such as real estate principles, practices, ethics, and legal regulations. It's essential to research and enroll in a program that aligns with your state's education hour prerequisites.

Background Checks and Criminal History

Another critical aspect of pre-licensing laws involves undergoing a background check which may include a specific type of fingerprinting and fees. Real estate commissions aim to ensure that individuals entering the industry possess the integrity and trustworthiness required to serve clients effectively. Be prepared to provide documentation and information necessary for this background check, and maintain transparency throughout the process. Understanding your state's criteria for the timing of this process and assessing criminal history is vital to anticipate any potential issues.

The State Exam

Passing the state exam is often the ultimate milestone in the pre-licensing journey. This comprehensive examination evaluates your understanding of real estate principles, regulations, and practices specific to your state. Adequate preparation, including study aids, practice exams, and a thorough review of relevant coursework, is essential to succeed in this crucial step.

Resourceful Navigation

Given the nuanced nature of pre-licensing laws and requirements, it's prudent to navigate this terrain with a resourceful mindset. Begin by visiting the official website of your state's Real Estate Commission. Here, you can find detailed information on pre-licensing requirements, application procedures, and study resources. This is an invaluable starting point to ensure you're on the right track.

Mentorship and Professional Guidance

Seek guidance from experienced mentors or real estate professionals who have successfully navigated the pre-licensing process in the state you are seeking licensure. Their insights and advice can provide valuable clarity and direction. Additionally, consider joining local real estate associations or networking groups to connect with industry peers who can offer clarity, guidance, and support.

Full comprehension and adherence to pre-licensing laws is an integral part of your journey toward becoming a licensed real estate agent. These laws lay the foundation for a successful and ethical career in real estate. By understanding your state's specific requirements, completing the necessary education hours, addressing background check criteria, and preparing diligently for the state exam, you set yourself up for success. Additionally, leveraging the guidance of mentors and industry professionals can further enhance your understanding and ensure a smooth path to licensure.

My Story: It's no secret, as stated before, that I had my husband to offer the answers I needed to navigate the initial pre-licensing process for the very first state I attained my real estate license. However, I also heavily relied on the Real Estate Commission's website. Then, after I enrolled in the real estate course with a live virtual instructor, I had the opportunity to get additional questions answered in real time as they arose.

Use your resources and ask lots of good questions!

Chapter Seven

Finding The Right Brokerage

The brokerage is yet another hot topic and step towards a successful career in real estate! Selecting the right brokerage is a BIG deal. As you begin your journey, it is important to find the right brokerage to affiliate your empire with. The brokerage you choose can have a significant impact on your success, career, and business satisfaction but not for the reasons many prospective agents think. In this chapter, we will discuss the benefits of finding the right brokerage the first time, things you should consider, and provide you with a few interview questions to ask brokers.

Getting it Right, Initially

First, let's talk about why it is important to find the right brokerage the first time. When you start your career in real estate (*depending on your state requirements*), you will be working under the supervision of a broker. The broker is responsible for providing you with the training and support you need to succeed. If you choose the wrong brokerage, you may not receive the support you need, which can lead to frustration and failure. You can always switch to a new brokerage if you are not getting what you need. However, it will cost additional time and dollars that you could have allocated to elevate your business, hence why it's best to find the right brokerage the first time.

On the other hand, if you find the right brokerage, you will receive the training and support you need to succeed to elevate and sustain your real estate business. You will have access to experienced agents and mentors who can provide you with guidance and advice. You will also have access to resources that can help you build your business, such as marketing materials and technology tools.

About Those Benjamins

Of course, you want to know about the compensation structure. However, before compensation, you need to focus on fit because if the brokerage doesn't align with your strategic goals, your compensation won't either.

Keep in mind that there is no set requirement for any brokerage's compensation model. In fact, your commission is 100% negotiable.

Each brokerage independently sets its agent compensation structure based on multiple factors. Commission could be a base salary, percentage, flat rate, or some other formula designated by the brokerage leadership. No matter what, make sure your commission structure is given to you in writing well before you officially affiliate your empire with a brokerage.

Let this formula sink in:

100% commission x $0 in closings
equals = $0 in income...plus fees.

Basically, no closings means no commission no matter how high of a split your brokerage offers. Therefore, as your top priority, buffer your budget and focus on selecting a brokerage with strong training, coaching, and a dedicated mentorship program to help you reach your strategic and SMART real estate goals through guidance and support. Because if you focus solely on the brokerage with top offering commission, but don't produce any closings...your commission will look very nice on paper, not your banking account.

Coaching and Mentoring

When you combine great coaching with your strong dedication and consistency, success becomes inevitable! AND...all of those fees many agents gripe about start to look smaller. Seek a brokerage that aligns with your values and provides support and mentorship opportunities to nurture your growth in the industry. Also...connect with your accountant to inquire how expenses impact your real estate business and the best way to set up your business (entity or not). You'll definitely thank me later.

Do Your Research

Before reaching out to brokerages, do your research. Get a clear understanding of the different types of brokerage structures. Talk to other agents, but don't set your decisions solely based on their opinion. Do your homework! I've seen agents across the country offer the most favorable opinions about a brokerage to only see their social posts announcing their new brokerage affiliation a month later while dragging *(criticizing)* their prior brokerage.

Know what excellence looks like for you. Your measurement of excellence might not be the same as another agent and if you are seeking excellence while they are content with fairness your goals will suffer based on their advice. Research to make the best decisions for your strategic goals. For example, some brokerages require in-person desk time while others are 100% remote. Know which style will flow seamlessly into your current schedule and lifestyle.

My Story: Many agents ask why I chose the brokerage I'm with until they recognize the connection between my last name and the brokerage's name. Yet it's still a very valid question. Now, I happened to build the brokerage I'm affiliated with based on research, our collective experiences in business, career, and real estate, in addition to our strategic goals.

Hands down, I am very aware of what good, great, and excellence look like for me so I used that as my compass. I also had the opportunity to gain a perspective from the information I ear-hustled from my husband's real estate experiences over the years, our strategic conversations, and other top producers real estate careers. Additionally, my professional background before real estate focused on developing and analyzing businesses, onboarding executive leadership, designing and executing SMART goals, and leading teams that guided my processes. I ultimately leaned into my experience to build and develop a brokerage with both a client and agent-centric focus. For the agents, from onboarding, training, and commission to closed deals, the focus is empowering real estate agents to achieve and exceed their desired level of success in a substantial way which bleeds into the service our clients receive.

When prospective agents and current agents are seeking to join my firm, call me to inquire, I want them to ask about our commission structure because what we offer is good. However, I'm more impressed by those who focus more on the culture of our brokerage, the training and mentoring we offer. Those are the agents who stand out the most and who I'm more apt to offer an invitation to join my brokerage. Those are also, the agents who seem to benefit the most from what our brokerage offers. rise to the top and the most fulfilled.

Interview Questions

Now, let's talk about some interview questions to ask brokers. These questions will help you determine if the brokerage is a good fit for you. Edit and evolve this list according to your strategic goals.

- What kind of training and support do you provide for new agents?
- How do you help agents build their business?
- What kind of technology tools do you provide for agents?
- Do you offer any marketing resources?
- What is your commission structure?
- How do you handle conflicts between agents?

- Are teams available and are agents required to join a team?
- What are the start-up, monthly, admin, transaction, annual, and other fees required?

You may have completed this step during your coursework as referenced in CHAPTER FOUR: *Real Estate School Exam: Effective Study Strategies and Prep*. If so, GREAT, you are a step ahead! If not, be sure to evaluate how your prospective brokerages line up with the four categories below and add additional categories that align with your individual goals and excellence.

Pro Tip: Use a planner like the *Hey...Future Real Estate Agents: Pro Planner* to organize your brokerage research responses.

1. Culture, Support, and Values

By initiating contact with potential brokerages, you can gauge the compatibility of their values, training programs, and company culture with your career goals and preferences while dually receiving clarification on course-related material. Some brokerages may offer study group sessions or a mentor while you are studying for your exam and continued mentorship after you pass and affiliate with the brokerage. This will also offer clues to help you discern the credibility of the information you find about the brokerage online and through other sources.

Pro Tip: Look beyond the numbers and big brand brokerage names and look into each brokerage's culture and values. Consider whether their mission aligns with your own goals and principles. A brokerage with a positive, collaborative, and supportive culture can significantly impact your success and career satisfaction.

2. Understanding Training Programs

Inquiring about a brokerage's training programs during your educational phase allows you to gain a deeper understanding of the support and resources they offer to new and veteran agents. This knowledge can influence your decision on which brokerage aligns best with your learning and professional development needs.

Inquire where, and when training is held to assess if the options will work for you. It's great to have robust training options but if they are only offered onsite at 10 am while you are tending to other responsibilities you will not reap the benefit. Some brokerages offer several training options while others may only offer one. Self-paced options will be pre-recorded and saved for your access at your convenience on a portal or drive. Some may track your progress and have regular live check-ins. Custom training options will be tailored to your learning style, specific needs, and strategic goals. In-person training will require onsite attendance and could be offered in a group or solo session. Virtual training will offer the option to train at any location, yet at a specific time designated by your broker or mentor.

3. Networking Opportunities: Building relationships with brokerages in advance can also expand your professional network whether you eventually decide to affiliate with the brokerage or not. Establishing rapport with brokerage representatives can lead to mentorship opportunities, valuable advice, and a smoother transition into the industry once you're licensed. Additionally, connecting with seasoned real estate professionals can provide valuable insights and support as you pursue your real estate aspirations.

4. Affiliation Requirements: Some brokerages may have specific requirements or preferences for new agents, such as post-licensing coursework, mentoring, and additional certifications. By establishing early contact, you can gather the information and potentially work on meeting these requirements in advance.

To Sum It Up, finding the right brokerage is an important part of building a successful career in real estate. Take the time to research and interview different brokerages to find the one that is the best fit for you. Remember, that finding the right brokerage the first time, will save you in time and money. As you evaluate each brokerage, be sure to consider culture, support, training, niche, and service area.

Chapter Eight

Budget Your Benjamins

The income potential in real estate is unlimited. At many points, the income may be overflowing while at other times it might not. Regardless, your winning potential is closely linked to your understanding of all of the costs associated with your real estate business. Expenses are an area where a lot of agents get themselves in trouble.

Let’s face it, although real estate agents have the opportunity to yield substantial income, the quantity, frequency, and consistency vary and are uncertain even for seasoned top producers. Additionally, there are several expenses that agents must budget to keep their license and manage their business. Many agents underestimate or are underinformed on this topic, so we will go deep in this section.

Expenses

Before diving into the real estate business as an agent, it's crucial to understand the associated costs comprehensively. Familiarize yourself with the financial aspects to ensure you are well-prepared for this exciting business. In preparation for your budget, you’ll need to create a comprehensive business plan that outlines your strategic goals, anticipated income, and expenses.

Start by researching the pre-licensing fees and course expenses required for obtaining your real estate license in your state(s). Remember, each state has its own set of rules and regulations so be sure you are focusing on the state(s) in which you want to get licensed. Consider the potential costs associated with joining your local real estate board and Multiple Listing Service (MLS). Contact various brokerages to explore their commission splits, transaction fees, Errors and Omissions (E&O) insurance, start-up, monthly, and annual fees. Take a closer look at different brokerage models, whether independent or franchised, to find the one that aligns with your overall goals. Don't sleep on independent or boutique brokerages; they often offer the best mentorship and broker access.

Food for Thought: Most states require Continuing Education to renew your license, so include the cost of those credits in your annual budget. However, some states also require post-licensing courses within 12-24 months of licensure, so make sure you know your state's requirements and the approximate cost of those courses.

Don't let the details scare you away from the business, take them in and get prepared. You can excel anywhere at any brokerage with the proper success set-up, strategic goals, execution, and consistency. However, mentorship and coaching programs will be crucial to your success. Therefore, be sure to understand how much coaching and mentorship is offered by each brokerage and by whom (a busy seasoned agent, dedicated mentor, or dedicated broker - it matters). A supportive and effective mentorship can be invaluable to your success, so weigh this factor carefully. If you love the brokerage and not the coaching, look into the costs of outside coaching/mentorship for agents and factor that cost into your preliminary budget.

Once you've started your real estate career, be prepared to allocate funds for marketing, technology (CRM), and recurring fees to maintain a robust presence in the market. A CRM is a Customer Relationship Manager. No, it's not a person, but if you get the right one and set it up properly, it will behave like your assistant. If your brokerage offers a CRM, keep in mind that you don't get to keep it if you leave, so factor the cost of a CRM into your budget, regardless. Get a deeper overview of CRM's in the next chapter!

Remember, while real estate is a rewarding career, it may require a substantial investment before your first commission check. Your first commission check may take a while to materialize as well.

Your First Deal!

Landing your first deal is exciting. However, closing your first deal is the absolute ultimate flex! So when it happens be sure to CELEBRATE!

While closing your first deal is exciting, barring a lengthy SOI (sphere of influence) list who already knows, likes, and trusts you as their Real Estate Agent and....is ready to buy or sell getting to that first deal and closing might take some patience. Overall strategy, execution, and consistency will be key because patience alone won't move the needle.

Listen, even if you landed a residential deal during your first week in the business, closing may take 4-8 weeks on average if it has no issues or delays (beyond your control). If you landed a commercial deal during your first week, a lease could take six months on average or 12 – 18 months for a sale. Those timeframes are averages; some deals close faster, and others may close much slower. Delays are typical in real estate transactions, and it takes many agents weeks, if not months, to get their first deal in motion, so be sure to keep this in mind to allow reasonable expectations.

The hard part, underneath the glamour of real estate, there is the struggle and the heartbreak. Not only are there delays in real estate... but there is also the fact that some deals, no matter how good they look, don't close. So as you prepare your income for the glitz and glamour, keep your budget real and consider the real-life situations that can impact your income when deals don't close, over and beyond your control.

Budgeting Strategies: Use a spreadsheet to track your income and expenses. Update it regularly as your business changes and make annual adjustments aligned with your business budget plan to accommodate your strategic goals. Your brokerage may also offer templates, workshops, and tools to aid you with your budget planning and tracking for your business.

Pro Budget Tip One: Initially, if possible, set aside 8 - 18 months of living and business expenses in a sub-account before you ditch all of your sources of income to become a full-time agent with no other income.

As a part-time agent with other income sources to fully support your living expenses, set aside 3-6 months of business expenses OR divide your total expenses by the year and set aside that amount monthly to ensure all of your real estate business expenses are taken care of on time without interrupting your lifestyle. This way, if you're a part-time agent with strategic goals to ditch your 9-5, you'll be ready at your own will, when your real estate business starts booming!

Pro Budget Tip Two: After you close your first deal each year, set aside all (if possible) of your mandatory real estate business expenses for the year in a subaccount. If setting aside all of your mandatory fees is not possible out of your first deal, consider setting aside those expenses out of your first few closings each year. Then in subsequent deals, consider setting aside 10% to 15% to cover marketing and career development expenses as you work to grow your business.

Same QR Code as before, more bonuses. If you didn't take the opportunity to grab your FREE for you resources...scan to grab your 12-month income and expense budget template!

MAKE IT SMART

Make your predictions about income make sense! It's great to have lofty goals, in fact, I encourage it as can challenge you to stretch and perform. However, be careful because there are several factors that must go into your goals in order for them to effectively materialize. For example, when you work on your initial and annual business plan, include a budget and marketing section that considers last year's market data, as well as predictive analytics, and most definitely make it SMART!

A SMART business plan is **S**pecific, **M**easurable, **A**chievable, **R**elevant, and **T**imebound. Align all of the elements of your business plan in a SMART way and your strategic goals will be too! Before you ink your goals question if each area is SMART. If your answer is yes, substantiate it. If your answer is no, make some adjustments until your goals get SMART. There is nothing more demotivating than goals that aren't achievable.

Additionally, a Realtor® which is a licensed Real Estate Agent who holds the Realtor® credential as a member of the National Association of Realtors®, has access to a wealth of tools. One recommended tool, in particular, is the Center for Realtor® Financial Wellness for additional tips and resources to aid in setting your business up to be financially well.

Side Note: Keep in mind that some brokerages require all of their licencees to hold the Realtor® credential while for other brokerages it's merely an option. Regardless to the brokerage, some Multiple Listing Systems (MLS) require all real estate agents and real estate brokers to hold the Realtor® credential to access their tools while others offer their subscription to all agents. Both the Realtor® credential and the MLS have *annual, monthly or quarterly expenses* that you'll need to consider in your budget if your brokerage, the MLS you subscribe to or some other resource requires you to hold the Realtor® credential.

Regardless of which tools you decide to use, it's essential to "*Budget your Benjamins*" wisely with buffers to help you and your real estate business stay financially sound before and after your first commission check. Financial preparedness will set you on the path to achieving elevated levels of success, affluence, and sustainability in this thriving industry.

Chapter Nine

9 Areas To Focus on After You're Licensed

After you've passed your real estate licensure exam, don't forget to celebrate that success first! Enjoy all of the kudos that go along with your accomplishment. Your path to licensure was hard work, the test may have felt like a twilight zone, but you did it! Next up, after you've affiliated with a brokerage or decided not (depending on your state's requirements) is to focus on specific areas to get your business off to the right start.

1 . Work on your business identity. Your business identity is your brand above and beyond your brokerage's brand. Your brand is what you say, how you say it, how people receive it, and how you look doing it--aka your image. Your brand, if created correctly, will effectively convey a unique message about your business, what sets you apart, who you serve, how well you service them, and attract your target audience. Your brand messaging may also encompass your niche market if you have definitively decided on one.

Your branding elements include:

- Mission
- Vision
- Value Proposition
- Logo
- Website
- Email
- Social Media presence
- Style
- Tone
- Business Cards
- , etc.

Your email address, for example, can also signal someone's perception of your professionalism. Perception is a reality in the eye of the beholder so, consider small details like your email address because sometimes a simple low-cost "*@yourname.com*" could make a difference. As another option, check with your brokerage, as some offer free email accounts (*i.e., yourname@burgosrealty.com*). Keep in mind that your brokerage's brand may need to be incorporated into your brand elements. Discuss branding requirements with your brokerage and follow your real estate commission's licensing rules before you finalize any branding designs.

2 . **Create a Business Plan with SMART Goals**: Set specific, measurable, achievable, relevant, and time-bound (SMART) goals for your real estate career. Goal-setting is crucial for maintaining focus and motivation throughout their journey. A comprehensive business plan will serve as your strategic roadmap. It should outline your target market, marketing strategies, budget, income goals, and growth plans.

A high percentage of millionaires arrived at that status by leveraging real estate. Further, most of the wealthiest people have at least 7 streams of revenue. How many streams of revenue will you include in your real estate business plan? Think about what wealth looks like for you and apply SMART goals to support and ignite the growth and wealth you are seeking.

3 . **Budget Your Time and Productivity:** Don't get busy, be productive! A business and career in real estate as an agent requires juggling various tasks and learning to prioritize and manage time efficiently. These elements are crucial for success. Evaluate how effectively you currently use your time and make adjustments that will offer adequate space for your real estate business. Add up the number of hours you are using throughout the day for everything, including sleep. Decide if Part-time or Full-time is right for you

and design a healthy balance of your personal life and real estate business.

Burnout is real, so it's essential to have a realistic understanding of your capacity, prioritize self-care, and maintain boundaries in your routine. Digital calendars and booking systems can be a time saver in business, don't overthink it. Use one! Budget your time, pop it on your calendar, and stick to it. You will appreciate this intel later.

4 . **Build Strong Relationships**: Client relationships are "kind of" a big deal in real estate. Building relationships with prospective clients, current clients, and real estate professionals as a business practice will take you far. Focus on building trust and rapport with your clients. Excellent customer service, follow-through, and follow-up can create extremely satisfied clients. Satisfied clients can become a significant source of repeat and referral business.

When considering the importance of relationships, know that people like to do business with professionals that they know, like, and trust. Think about the businesses you engage with and what drives you to do business with them, then replicate that idea for your business.

5 . **Network to Build Your Net Worth.** Embody an attitude of collaboration over competition and win together! Connect with industry professionals who will enhance your expertise and expand your business. Real estate developers and contractors, real estate attorneys, mortgage lenders, credit repair specialists and investors, and other real estate agents are a good start. Don't forget to network with business professionals outside of real estate as well!

Pro Tip: Connect with agents who don't service your service area or state, create an intentional partnership, and they'll become a source of referral income for you. Also, when diversifying your network outside of real estate, PTA's, Rotary, and Chamber of Commerce are great options as a starting point. You'll thank me later!

6 . Handling Rejections and Challenges: OH! MY...this is a big one! Just like success, rejections, and challenges will happen. Find a way to empower yourself through rejections. Take the "L" - the love in the learning and understand that each rejection brings you closer to your acceptance. Prepare for the realities of the real estate industry, including potential rejections and challenges.

Keep in mind that It's very possible to turn a frown upside down. Receiving a "no" might not be the end of the conversation. Explore why you are receiving a rejection or why a challenge exists. Consider if you presented with excellence. Did you lean in with your value front and center? Not with arrogance but instead from a position of solving a pain point that your client is actually experiencing.

Regardless of how poised you show up, It won't take long before you face rejection or a challenge. The real estate business is filled with several of them. Although some will, many won't have any connection to the way you performed. Don't get discouraged, as challenges present an opportunity for you to seize the moment. So, pick your head up and lead like a value-offering rockstar to overcome those situations. Listen to the challenge being presented and use your expertise to find an adequate solution in favor of your client or prospective client.

No matter what the result, activate your resilience and optimism, and breathe because you cannot do anything without oxygen anyway! Then eliminate the opportunity for "no's" and go get your "yes's"!

7 . Continue Your Education and Professional Development: Some states also require licensees to take post-licensing courses and successfully pass an exam with a proctor present. Most states require real estate agents to take annual or biennial continuing education credits. Above and beyond what is required, continuous learning and professional development are integral to your long-term success. Attend real estate seminars, workshops, and conferences to stay up to date with industry trends and enhance your knowledge and position as an expert. This industry tends to shift abruptly (*remember 2008 and 2020*), and while it usually stays lucrative, you want to be ready to pivot when the industry shifts.

Pro Tip: After you get a handle on your real estate business, level up! Research certifications and designations that will accentuate your skill set and niche or your expertise as a buyer's agent. You can find these requirements for many reputable certifications and designations on the National Association of Realtors® website. Some designations and certifications whether they are mentioned on the National Association of Realtors® website or not require agents to hold the Realtor® credential, while others may not. Be sure to confirm the eligibility requirements of a designation or certifications before you lean into it.

8 . Leverage Technology: The effective use of technology will help you multi-task and move your business further faster and sometimes while you are asleep. Don't run away from technology. Embrace it and take the necessary steps to figure it out. A tech-savvy agent can streamline their operations, build effective systems, and enhance client experiences leveraging the right technology for their business.

If the idea of technology just made you lose your cookies--don't worry. You're not alone; many agents fear this area. However, a solid broker, mentor, or coach will walk you through all of the technology resources that will be key for your business, from CRM systems to transaction management, virtual tours, and social media marketing. If you can pass that real estate exam (no matter how many tries) you can master technology. You Got This!

9 . Office Set-Up and Equipment: The fun stuff...the office! If you're working in a traditional real estate brokerage, you may have the opportunity to secure a workspace or office at their location. If not, you'll need to find a quiet dependable space to work. In this business it's very easy to set up a workspace at home, but what happens when you need to meet clients? No worries; there are several options depending on your state and brokerage rules. You can potentially meet clients online via Zoom, at public places like coffee/tea shops, libraries, or at co-working spaces but do follow all pertinent rules and regulations regarding meeting clients. And...don't forget to take any and all safety precautions required or recommended by your brokerage.

What about closings? Well...they often take place at the attorney or title company's office, in rare cases, they may take place at the real estate brokerage's official business office. When your office is required, talk to your broker about your in-office options at your brokerage.

When you are not out with clients, in the field networking, or prospecting (if you haven't invested in an assistant or transaction coordinator yet or have one on your team), you'll spend a lot of time juggling between your phone and computer. Regardless of your situation, today's technology makes working in real estate simpler than it was years ago and therefore you can use your smartphone for many of your tasks. However, having a dependable laptop with cloud-based tools (see below) coupled with your smartphone will make managing your business easier.

Yet another bonus...scan the QR code to get a FREE quick list of recommended equipment for real estate agents.

My Office Set-up Story: As a brokerage owner, I have several offices to work from in several states--not bragging, but stick with me for my point. Although I do work in the office, I prefer my home setup. Everything is where I need it, when I need it, and when it's time to shift gears into mom mode, I can easily do so without a commute. Additionally, when I need to work late (often), I'm already home, so it's not a challenge to get dinner on deck, my youngest tucked into bed, and get back to finishing my workday...down the hall. Working at home doesn't always work for me but when it does, it's fantastic!

I meet most of my clients via Zoom when we don't need to meet in person. When we need to meet in person, it's usually on-site for showings or property walk-thrus. My clients love the flexibility and efficiency of connecting with me online when it makes sense versus scheduling an in-person meeting every time and bonus... they still get to see my face! Overall, when it makes sense, online meetings save their time, and mine too!

Although I have a computer in the office, I do use my laptop and iPad (with keyboard) the most. They give me the greatest opportunity to work on the go especially when clients, inspectors, or appraisers are late for their appointments or during open houses.

Pro-Tip: No matter where you work (at home or in the office) strategically get outside. Change up your environment and pop into a local coffee/tea shop, eatery, co-working, or other place where you can set up your laptop and meet people. Wear your branded apparel, badge, or something that says..“HEY...I 'm a Real Estate Agent” (see what I did there) and connect with people. Since this is not a book on lead generating I'll stop here (stay tuned), but you get the point.

Oh and if you need some “HEY...*I'm a Real Estate Agent*” apparel, scan that QR Code that's floating throughout this book.

To Sum It Up, business in general, and especially the real estate business is a numbers game. The agent that effectively conveys their brand in a convincing way to the most people connected to their target audience wins. Your professional presence is essential, people need to see you, know you, like you, and trust you. The way to accomplish that is to present an effective brand, get outside and showcase your expertise, use technology to aid with speed and efficiency, and tell the world about what you do--don't keep your business a secret!

Align all of the nine steps in this chapter with your goals to set your path in the right direction after you're licensed.

Chapter Ten

Wait...What? Systems?

In the fast-paced and dynamic world of real estate, where success is driven by strategy and execution, setting up effective systems is your secret weapon. I've learned that systems are the backbone of a thriving real estate business. Since I said the "S" word, let's dive deeper into what systems really are and why they're crucial for your journey to becoming a successful real estate agent.

Systems protect your standards and although in some cases, they might initially require an extra step or two, they are excellent for helping you work smarter not harder in your business. In the context of real estate, a system refers to organized and repeatable processes that agents establish to streamline operations. Systems are processes, policies, and procedures designed to help manage various aspects of your real estate business with efficiency, consistency, and professionalism. Systems create a structured framework that guides your day-to-day activities, ensuring that you and or your team don't miss a beat.

What's In A System Anyway?

Consistency: Consistency is vital in real estate. Whether handling client inquiries, managing listings, or conducting property showings, having well-defined systems ensures that you deliver a consistent experience to each of your clients every time.

Time Management: As a real estate agent, time is your most valuable asset. Systems help you optimize your time by providing step-by-step guidelines for tasks, enabling you to work smarter and accomplish more in less time. We take a deeper dive into this extremely important topic in the next chapter.

Client Satisfaction: Providing exceptional customer service is a hallmark of successful agents. Systems help you stay on top of communication, follow-ups, and client needs, ensuring your clients feel supported and valued. Systems will also force you to collect those good reviews from satisfied clients who have experienced your sound systems. Which will in turn drive more business your way!

Efficiency: With systems in place, you can handle tasks more efficiently. You'll waste less time figuring out what needs to be done next and more time focusing on tasks that directly impact your business growth. Additionally, mastering efficiency aids you with reducing errors and ultimately getting things right early on in your business and transactions.

Scale and Growth: Maintaining high standards becomes challenging without effective systems as your business expands. Systems allow you to scale your operations without sacrificing quality, enabling you to handle a larger volume of transactions and potentially manage a larger team.

Reduced Stress: Real estate can be stressful, especially without proper organization. Systems help reduce stress by providing clear guidelines for each task, reducing the likelihood of mistakes and oversights. In addition, your systems will give you time to take much-needed breaks that afford the space you need to return refreshed and motivated to achieve or exceed your strategic goals.

Compliance: There are many rules and regulations to follow as an agent at the state, federal, and local levels. In addition, you'll have rules to follow for your brokerage and your LLC (if you have one), and taxes, to name a few. How you complete contracts, which tools you use, who needs to sign at the brokerage and client level, and when these steps happen are all part of a system. Efficient compliance systems will help you keep your priorities in order and you out of hot water.

Different Types of Systems in Real Estate

You can develop systems for every facet of your real estate business. To get your juices flowing, here is a short list of areas you may need to create systems for ultimate efficiency in your business.

Buyer Processes: Create a step-by-step system for guiding buyers through hiring other real estate professionals like attorneys and title companies, when and how property inspections, showings, offers, negotiations, and closing logistics, should happen. Within this system, you'll want to consider who does what, when, and what documents if any are needed for compliance and record keeping. Your Buyer systems will keep your clients informed and engaged at every stage and any team members involved in the transaction from assistants to transaction coordinators.

Client Communication: Set up systems for regular communication with clients, updating them on market trends, new listings, and other relevant information. Within many of your systems, you might also include a section for a communication system with your client and team for each of the steps of the transaction. Additionally, you can create a client communication section for the various types of communication to your client. Some examples might include your welcome, client contract, offer communication, pre-closing communication, post-closing communication, follow-up, and general touch points to stay in touch.

Lead Generation: A well-defined system for lead generation helps identify potential clients and engage with them properly and promptly. Develop a system to manage leads from identifying, cultivating, and stewarding. Behave like an absolute pro and create an automated follow-up process to add your leads to ensure that no lead is left behind. Set up a rating system to organize the communication that goes to each lead.

Listing Management: From listing agreements to listing marketing plans, having a system for managing listings ensures that each property is marketed effectively and consistently. Much like your Buyer system, your listing management system will keep the seller informed of the elements of a transaction, what to expect, timelines to adhere to, and more. Additionally, when other team members from marketing to assistants or transaction coordinators are involved, your listing management system will help them perform according to your standards.

Marketing and Branding: Strategic marketing efforts; including social media posting, email campaigns, and content creation. Consistent branding across all channels aligned with your mission, vision, and value proposition is a vital system. Remember, affiliated agents may need to include their brokerage's branding and or contact information within their branding so know the rules and build marketing and branding systems to comply with your licensure state and brokerage rules.

Networking and Relationship Building: Establish a system for building and nurturing relationships with other real estate professionals and potential clients. Include your frequency of connection and which tools (attending events, volunteering, joining or creating networking groups, etc.) you'll use to support this system. Your follow-up management should also be a part of this system. Follow-up management could be as simple as a combination of a call every quarter, text message check-ins every month, a card or note in the mail, or intentional invites to chat over lunch, coffee, or tea. Whatever you decide, create a networking and relationship-building system that makes sense for your business.

You might not want to invite a stranger you are soliciting to get their listing out to eat as that can become costly (considering you'd do this for every prospect) and might not be the best use of your time. And...in some cases, creepy and unsafe might I add. However, depending on your budget you might consider hosting an ice cream social in partnership with a local ice cream shop (whom you've built a relationship with) at a park within your target area. Again, make it make sense, know your area, and follow all rules and regulations because this idea won't work everywhere.

Personnel Management: Generate a system that details who you hire, when and why, their level of access, their overall job description, and how they are to do their job. Additionally, for affiliated agents, many states require that the brokerage is involved at some level when it comes to hiring staff. Therefore, your personnel management will need to consider any brokerage requirements. Lastly, if you've created an entity for your business, you might have other compliance requirements to adhere to so be aware and consider all avenues before adding personnel.

Transaction Coordination and Management: A transaction coordination and management system helps you manage all the paperwork, deadlines, and communication involved in a real estate transaction. However, the transaction management software would be a tool that an agent might use within their system. Some agents hire a transaction coordinator for their transaction management, but the best way to ensure efficiency is to create a system first regardless of if you are managing your transactions or if you've hired a coordinator.

For each one of your systems, do not forget to follow up. Set yourself apart. Many agents neglect to allocate space within their systems for follow-up which can be the difference between securing a client, retaining a client or not. Additionally, Consider which tools you will include to optimize your systems for consistency and ease of management.

To Sum It Up, work smarter, not harder with effective systems! The key to successful systems is adaptability. Your systems should make managing your real estate business easier. As the real estate market evolves, your systems should evolve too. Regularly review and update your processes to ensure they remain effective and aligned with industry trends and your business needs. By incorporating proven systems into your real estate journey, you'll be setting yourself up for success. These systems will not only help you navigate the complexities of the real estate industry but also differentiate you as a professional who operates with precision and excellence.

Chapter Eleven

CRM

Customer Relationship Management

You've absorbed a lot of information thus far and now it's time to talk about CRM's. In this chapter, we'll discuss the key features to look for when selecting the right CRM for your business needs. There are many acronyms in real estate, but one that you will hear and use most often is called a CRM. A CRM, or Customer Relationship Management system. It is an essential tool for any real estate agent looking to build and maintain a successful business. Big emphasis on tool!

To avoid confusion as you move forward in your real estate career, know that CRM's although referenced as systems earlier are technically tools, not systems. CRM's are tools agents can use to complement their systems. Tools and systems are two of the most commonly yet incorrectly interchanged words in the industry. They are NOT the same. Systems are processes or procedures (workflows) that you will follow to efficiently run every aspect of your business. Whereas tools are used to aid in the efficiency of systems like CRM's, transaction management software, and more. Now that we have that untangled, let's dive into this chapter.

First and foremost, it's important to consider the user interface. Let's be clear, not all CRM's are built the same and neither is your technical savvy. So be sure to select a CRM that is intuitive and comfortably within your technical ability. After all, you should use it on a daily basis, so it should be something that you enjoy using. Make sure that the CRM you choose has a user-friendly interface that makes it easy to input and track client data.

Another important feature to consider is automation. A good CRM should be able to automate many of the repetitive tasks that come with managing a large client base. Look for features like automated lead capture, follow-up reminders, task automation, and campaign management. This will save you time and simplify your efficiency.

Integration is also crucial. Make sure that the CRM you choose integrates with other tools that you use regularly, such as your email, e-blast tool, mass texting tool, and calendar for example. This will help you stay organized and ensure that all of your client data is easy to find in a centralized space.

Finally, consider the reporting capabilities of the CRM. Seek out a system that can provide detailed reports that include analytics on your clients, such as their buying and selling history, preferences, and contact information. This will allow you to make more informed decisions and better serve your clients. AND...don't forget about support! Consider your technical ability and the ease of resolving issues if the system goes down or you actually find a way to break it! Don't worry; the chances of you breaking the system are extremely slim, but just to be safe, make sure the CRM you purchase has decent support available at hours when you'd likely use the tool.

My Story: In one of my prior careers, I had to focus on large data sets with various databases that didn't speak to each other. In the same career while at another organization my team and I had the pleasure of creating multiple Excel spreadsheets with complicated formulas to track data points across the organization to make all of the data make sense. It was grueling and partially because of those traumatic experiences, I'm very selective about my real estate CRM.

I've tested several and there isn't one that does everything I need it to do but many get close enough so my focus, when it comes to CRM's is the usability. How user-friendly is it, how it masters many of the boxes I want checked, whether I'll actually use it, and how cost-efficient the tool is are some of the areas I analyze. I don't mind spending top dollar (within budget) for something that simplifies business for me in a way that frees up time and makes my systems flow easier, but it has to pass my make-it- make-sense test.

To Sum It Up, choosing the right CRM is essential for any real estate agent looking to build a successful business. Keep the key features mentioned here in mind and create your own based on your needs when selecting your CRM. Do that and you'll be well on your way to success with fewer headaches!

More FREE info! Scan QR code to get access to a list of my CRM top picks! It's the same code as before so if you scanned it earlier, you're already ahead!

Chapter Twelve

Time Management: The Money and Sanity System

Mastering Time Management in Real Estate

In the fast-paced real estate industry, effective time management is more than a skill; it's a necessity. The more efficiently an agent manages their time, the greater of a chance they have to make and exceed their earning potential. Understanding the highest and best use of your time forges productivity. As a prospective real estate agent preparing to embark on this exciting career journey, you'll soon realize that your ability to manage time efficiently will directly impact your success and minimize stress. In this chapter, we'll dive deep into the art of time management specifically tailored to the real estate business as an effective system with some juicy nuggets that can be drawn from my personal story.

Time Crunch: Real Estate's Unique Challenge

Real estate is a unique industry that doesn't adhere to traditional 9-to-5 hours. It operates on a more flexible schedule, often dictated by client needs and market demands. As a result, mastering time management in real estate requires a different approach compared to many other professions. Let's take a closer look at why time management is crucial for your real estate success.

Client-Centric Industry: Real estate revolves around your clients' schedules. They may require your assistance during evenings, weekends, or even holidays. Although you get to set your schedule, being responsive and available when clients need you is a hallmark of excellent service. It is essential to be available (you or someone on your team) for your client base when they are available. Just remember, you are in control of your availability. You are in control of the clients you decide to work with. If an appointment doesn't fit in your schedule, you don't have to accept it. If a client is only available when you are not, you can offer provisions through another team member or refer them to another agent.

Varied Tasks: Real estate agents wear many hats. You'll juggle tasks such as prospecting, lead generation, property showings, negotiations, paperwork, marketing, and more. In addition, if you've taken note of my secret go-pro sauce then learning continuously will be on the list with those mentioned tasks. Efficiently allocating time to each of these tasks and knowing when to hire and delegate support is vital to an agent's sustainability.

Market Dynamics: Real estate markets can fluctuate rapidly. Being able to adapt your schedule, approach, and target to capitalize on market opportunities or navigate market challenges is crucial for success. An agent who allocates small bites of time to stay abreast of the market shifts through daily analysis will be well-positioned to adapt accordingly.

The Foundation and System: Goal Setting

Effective time management starts with clear yet SMART goals. Before you dive into managing your time, take a moment to define objectives for your real estate business. Your goals might include:

- Achieving a specific number of transactions per month or year.

- Earning a specific income level.

- Expanding your network and client base.

- Enhancing your expertise in a particular area or niche, such as luxury properties or commercial real estate.

Once you've set your goals, make sure they pass the SMART test and then break them down into smaller, actionable steps. Those steps should consider what the task is, how often it needs to be completed, who needs to be involved, and when it should get done. Additionally, knowing what defines success for your goal and the ability to measure that success will be key indicators to determine if your goal is actually SMART. This will make it easier to allocate your time to the tasks that directly contribute to achieving these goals.

Tools and Systems: Time Management Techniques

In your real estate career, you'll encounter various time management techniques and tools. Here are some tried-and-true methods to help you make the most of your time:

Prioritization: Start your day by identifying your most important tasks. Technically, this should be done weekly and only tweaked as your priorities shift. For example, a closing date change or a new client ready to buy or sell. The activities you prioritize will have the most significant impact on your business. Focus on completing these tasks before addressing less critical matters.

Time Blocking: Allocate specific blocks for production strides on different tasks. For example, reserve the morning for lead generation, prospecting, and following up on deliverables, the afternoon for client meetings and property showings, and the evening for administrative work and marketing. Be diligent with your time blocks to include specific blocks of time for responding to emails, returning phone calls, and engaging on social media throughout the day to stay on top of your communication without allowing it to consume your day.

To-Do Lists: Maintain a daily or weekly to-do list. This can be digital or physical. List all the tasks you need to complete and check them off as you finish each one. It provides a sense of accomplishment and helps you stay organized. Often, seeing your productivity can encourage you to be more productive.

Calendar Management: Set it so you don’t forget it. Use digital calendars to schedule appointments, meetings, and important deadlines. Set reminders to ensure you never miss a critical event or task.

Time and Project Management Apps: Explore time management apps and tools designed to help you track your activities, screen time, and water intake (yes, that's a thing), manage your schedule, monitor individual and team projects, and improve your overall organization and productivity.

Pro Tip: Budget an online digital booking tool into your expenses, you'll thank me later. There are quite a few free options as well. Regardless, find one that offers automation, workflows, and syncs with your calendar (personal and business). Be diligent about setting up booking links and add the link to your email signature, website (if you have one), landing pages, and social media. This way, your clients and business associates can book time with you at their convenience when you are available. This saves time juggling between parties when trying to find a feasible time to meet.

My Story: When my oldest child was in her mid-single digits, she realized the importance of seeing productivity and how that encouraged her to complete the tasks on her to-do list. I vividly remember the evening she figured that out. Many tears were shed, but she got there. She was overwhelmed by the idea that she had to clean up the tornado she made in her room, by herself. Putting things back after she was done with them wasn't actually a thing yet for her, hence the tornados. But this one was a much bigger one than normal. She just couldn't fathom how she'd get it done, it seemed absolutely impossible.

As much as the mom in me was melting and wanted to help her, it was time that she understood how to manage her space so she'd have more time to do things she enjoyed. Therefore, beyond advice on a technique and my usual encouragement, I didn't offer any manual assistance. She was pacing back and forth around the room in the most non-productive way. Picking up one thing and racing it across the room the zig-zag continued with waterfalls until I suggested that she pick a section, work on that, check it off, and move to another. After a few more tears, she decided to take my advice. Section by section, she got it done.

Even today as an adult, she still uses that technique although I believe she creates fewer tornados than she did in her mid-single digits. She recalls how that day changed the way she organizes things that feel overwhelming. She decided to manage her time in a way so that she sees productivity as she moves through her day, week, month, etc. Like that day, chipping away at big chunks of her goals, section by section gives her a sense of accomplishment and relief that inspires her to continue moving forward.

There are days when we both feel overwhelmed by the massive amount of things on our to-do lists, along with the unexpected things that come up in business. Beyond prayer, there is a sequence of two questions we use to reset ourselves.

Q: How are we going to get this done? **A**: Section by section!

Q: How are we going to eat that elephant? **A**: In bite-sized pieces!

Find and create efficient tools and systems to guide your path through effective time management.

Client Management: Balancing Act

In real estate, client management plays a pivotal role in time management. Building strong relationships with clients while efficiently handling their needs is a delicate balance. Ensuring that you or someone on your team is available when they are and managing their expectations of your availability is key. Here's how to master this aspect of time management:

Communication: Set clear expectations with clients regarding your availability and preferred communication methods. Let them know when you'll be available, away on vacation, and when appropriate when you'll be unresponsive or slower to respond for some time. Be responsive and keep them informed about important developments.

Automate When Possible: Use technology to automate routine tasks. Set up email templates for frequently sent emails such as a client welcome, or steps of the transaction like attorney review or clear to close. Set up autoresponders to let people know you are away and when you'll respond to their message or who they can contact for emergencies. Let them know you received their message and approximately how soon (hours) you will get back to them if you can commit to a timeframe. This might reduce the stream of duplicate emails, calls, or text messages you receive before you're able to return the message. Your CRM (Customer Relationship Management) system can automate and help streamline many of your client interactions.

Delegate: Recognize when it's appropriate to delegate tasks to others, such as administrative work or property inspections. Delegating allows you to focus on high-value activities. Delegate a trusted team member (if you have one) to respond to emergencies or major accounts while you are away on vacation or have a full day of meetings.

Market Savvy: Adapting to Real Estate Trends

In the ever-evolving real estate industry, staying informed about market trends and adapting your strategies accordingly is crucial.

Here's how to integrate market awareness into your time management:

Continuous Learning: Dedicate time for ongoing education and professional development. Stay up-to-date with industry trends, legal updates, and technological advancements. As a real estate agent, adopting a mindset of continuous learning will serve you well as the industry and your market can change quickly.

Networking: Allocate time for networking events, both online and in person. Building and maintaining a robust professional network can lead to valuable opportunities. It cannot be emphasized enough that people like to do business with other people whom they know, like, and trust so get outside and meet your prospective clients and partners at networking events.

Market Analysis: Regularly analyze local market conditions. This insight can help you adjust your marketing and pricing strategies to align with current trends. Market analysis sits in a category by itself because it's so important yet it directly connects with continuous learning. If you really want to stay on top of your market include time on your calendar to study what is happening in your market(s) daily. I'm pretty sure that you'll thank me later.

My Story: Even as an employee of a company, I had to block time on my calendar to expand my knowledge and contribute to my career development. Those time blocks were weekly and came in the form of webinars, networking meetings, and sitting with other staff members to better understand their programs and management or industry training and certifications. Unless there was an urgent need that could not wait until my weekly designated hour was complete, I did not avail myself during that window. When possible, I connected those windows to my lunch hour to ensure I'd have the uninterrupted time I needed.

As an entrepreneur in real estate, that theme stands true today. During my annual business planning, I allocate SMART goals for development which include what I need and want to learn throughout the year and any certifications or designations I plan to achieve. Then as I focus on the "T" (timely/timebound) in SMART, I put the completion and or course dates on my digital calendar before the start of the year. This system helps to ensure that I stick to my educational goals and it diversifies my accomplishments so I don't only end the year with an abundance of work completed or pending projects.

Managing Stress: The Time Management Paradox

Efficient time management not only enhances your productivity but also reduces stress. However, it's important to recognize that excessive stress can hinder your time management efforts. Here's how to strike a balance:

Stress Management Techniques: Incorporate stress-reduction practices into your routine. Meditation, exercise, and mindfulness can help you stay focused and calm, even during hectic periods.

Time for Reflection: Periodically review your time management strategies and adjust them as needed. Reflect on what's working and what's not, and be willing to make changes. Review your productivity to confirm if you are off or on target. Seeing your productivity or lack thereof will offer a realistic view of where you are, how you feel, and what (if any) adjustments need to be made.

Manage Expectations: Let your clients and team know when you will and will not be available. Let them know when they can reasonably expect a response, information they requested, or a completed project. Regularly communicate when changes to those commitments may occur. When a client or team member's expectations are beyond your capacity, communicate what will reasonably work for your availability.

Time for Yourself: Add yourself to your calendar. Remember that an effective time management system isn't just about work and your client's needs. It's also about maintaining a healthy work-life balance or blend. Allocate time to elevate your knowledge or for personal activities, relaxation, and self-care to avoid burnout and protect your physical and mental health.

Pro Tip: Although it is impossible to make more time, it is possible you can find time that you aren't using well. Scrutinize your schedule and when you take certain actions. Analyze how you are spending your or wasting it and reallocate inefficiencies. Consider where you can effectively multi-task.

Find Time

People find time for the things that they enjoy and find most valuable. Therefore, if you find having a real estate business enjoyable and or valuable, you'll hunker down and find the necessary time to get your license, set up your business, and achieve your strategic goals. For some, that might mean making small easy tweaks or difficult drastic adjustments. Whichever category you might fall in, focus on your goal and you will find the value.

Have an honest look at your strategic goals and how much time you are going (not trying) to apply to get there daily. A few small steps each day can lead to a BIG accomplishment at the end of a season. That elephant is not so big when you take it on in small bites. Start with the end of a week, month, quarter, or year, and decide what you want your look-back period to look or feel like. What do you actually want to have completed? Think about this in a SMART way. For example: if you want to make 7 figures, great, I love that goal! How many streams of revenue do you need to activate to get there and how much time will that cost you in daily bite-sized pieces? Do you need to make adjustments to your current schedule?

Consider some of these suggestions:

Have a podcast on your schedule? Consider listening while managing other tasks like driving to and from the office, working, walking, preparing the kid's lunches, or during solo mealtimes (if that's a thing).

Have a favorite show you just have to watch? I get it, I do too! Consider watching it while you cook or clean. You get something off your list and your show. However, be careful because some of that time is also time that you could effectively reallocate to listening to an educational podcast or watching an educational webinar related to your real estate test prep or business.

Do you take your lunch break every day? You really should. When you do, break your lunch hour into 3 categories, meal, refresh, and execute. 15 minutes eating, 15 minutes renewing your mind, and 30 minutes executing a task that helps you move the needle to get to the next level. Follow this formula and you'll not only ensure you're taking time for yourself but you'll also be closer to achieving one of your personal goals regularly.

Rest is important for everyone, especially for an entrepreneur. Make sure you are getting regular and sufficient rest. While rest is important analyze how effectively you rest to ensure you are not wasting time tossing and turning. Also, consider if you have the ability and capacity to wake up an hour or so earlier. Fill that hour with something that fills you like prayer, exercise, reading, or meditation.

Give yourself grace and breaks, but be honest about how you are using your time and how you can use it more effectively. Then make changes where necessary and you'll find time in such a way that you might feel like you are making it.

My Story About Time: Being a mom, it's hard to talk about time without considering how I use it as a parent. Like parenting, time management is a life-long learning process. You never stop managing time, just as once you receive the title, you never stop being a parent. You nail time management and yet some form of turbulence sneaks in like extreme fatigue, school, career change, wait...umh...a baby or two, a fun night con mucho vino (too much wine), age, stress or mood shifts your course. Eventually, (baring extreme circumstances) when the goal holds excitement, unwavering value, or the New Year's resolutions roll in, you'll adjust your habits and discern new ways to eliminate the obstacle (not the baby...sheesh) or work around it to get back on the productivity track.

My Relationship with Time

When it comes to my relationship with time, I need to feel good about my efficacy which includes my family while not excluding myself (work in progress on the self part). I need to accomplish some major and minor milestones within a reasonable period of time. Additionally, my time needs to be efficiently sorted with a blend of personal and professional milestones while managing short-term goals and dually taking small bites of long-term goals. How do you eat the elephant? In bite-sized pieces.

How It Started

I've learned I am my most effective being when I consistently awake in the silence of the dark (in color) morning around 4am to pray and exercise. I realized this when my oldest child was a baby. When she awoke, she required so much of my time and I absolutely loved it! On other mornings, she was masterful in wrestling up a full-on hurricane, but that's a story for another book or a chat over tea.

However, even though I loved her morning sunshine, I felt like I was on a hampster wheel at times --BUSY, but never really accomplishing anything substantial. I also was not starting my day in a way that sincerely filled me as a person before I took on the rest of the world. Often, I'd feel depleted before the day was near an end. When I recognized that I was in control of my outcome, I made tweaks to the way I entered and managed my days and things changed for the better.

My Shift In Perspective

For one, my perspective shifted when I realized it was necessary to fill my cup and put my life vest on first. I refocused from a lens that would ensure my daughter's needs and wants were met yet not sacrificing mine. I analyzed what I needed to feel full because pouring from a half-full space depleted my tank incessantly. Ultimately, she needed me to operate from a full space, heck she needed me to operate from overflow while I did too. She needed reliable routines, structure, and boundaries, yet access to me, and so did I.

Beyond her needing a mom that was consistently operating from a full space, (*because I hadn't mastered overflow yet*), she had the necessities. However, with my new understanding of the synergy of our needs, I made tweaks without guilt. Some were simple like adjusting her bedtime by 30 minutes, which helped to set up efficient time boundaries for both of us. Listen, those extra 30 minutes or so at night added a valuable amount of quiet time to rest my mind and reset for the next day before I was too exhausted to think coherently. I adjusted my sleep schedule, went to bed at a reasonable time, and woke up refreshed two hours earlier than I had prior. Those two hours helped position me to operate from overflow before my daughter woke up with her weather center. Now, when she awoke, I was ready for her sunshine or hurricane. Not only was I prepared for my day and the weather she delivered, but I also experienced a fully me-centered morning including exercise, prayer, planning and sometimes reading all without any interruption!

My Extra Time and Overflow!

And just like that...(do the math) I effectively positioned myself to operate from a space of overflow by reallocating 17.5 hours per week and finding a hidden 70 hours a month in my schedule! Years later, I found another 10 hours by using my lunch hour more effectively. I realized I didn't need a full hour to eat although taking a break was necessary. I ate my lunch efficiently aligned with my strategic goals. A portion of my lunch hour became a valuable proofreading time while completing my undergraduate degree and as I embarked on graduate studies because saving that task to the evening, when I was the most exhausted would not showcase any sensible written words for me.

A Work In Progress

By the time I embarked on my real estate business, I was several businesses, volunteer leadership positions, a husband, and a couple of kids deep. At the very least, at this point in my life, I can say time management was always a work in progress. Some days I undeniably master it and others I have to try again and double up the next day. However, monitoring my time and the adjustments I make ensure that I operate from a full cup and give from my overflow is the compass that affords the space for me to be present, happy, and meet my strategic goals.

Your Time, Your Success

Unlike money, the one thing you cannot get back or make more of is time. Like money, it's critical to utilize your time wisely to avoid wasting it. Time management is the key to every successful real estate career. It enables you to provide exceptional service to your clients, adapt to market dynamics, and maintain a healthy work-life blend. Emphasis on healthy! As you embark on your journey as a real estate agent, remember that mastering time management is not a one-time task but an ongoing process. With dedication and practice, you can ensure that your time is an asset, not a limitation, in your pursuit of real estate success. Remember, time waits for no one and if you don't manage it, you'll waste it.

Scan here to grab a list of some of my favorite CRM, Organization and Time Management top picks!

Chapter Thirteen

Independent Contractor vs. Employee

In real estate, understanding the distinction between being an independent contractor and an employee is essential for prospective agents. These two classifications represent distinct working arrangements with different implications for your career. In most cases, real estate agents operate as independent contractors. However, there are some niche roles like property management or inside sales agents for large contractors or companies (for example) in which licensed real estate agents might operate as employees and receive a salary.

Independent Contractor

There is a mental mind shift that is necessary when operating as an independent contractor. Real estate agents who operate as independent contractors are actually a business. Some real estate agents have the opportunity (depending on the state) to set up a business entity, such as an LLC, to collect compensation. An LLC is a business entity that provides additional protections for businesses that a sole proprietorship does not, as well as tax opportunities for benefits. Check with your accountant, tax advisor, broker, or real estate commission to confirm and get specifics for your state.

Flexibility and Autonomy: As an independent contractor, you essentially run your own business within the brokerage. You have the freedom to set your work hours, determine your marketing strategies, and manage your client relationships. This autonomy is one of the primary draws for many real estate agents.

Commission-Based Compensation: Independent contractors typically earn commissions based on their real estate transactions. This means you'll only get paid when you successfully close a deal. It can be a high-risk, high-reward setup, as your income is directly tied to your sales performance.

Business Expenses: Independent contractors are responsible for covering their business expenses, including marketing costs, office space (if not provided by the brokerage), and any other tools or resources needed to conduct their real estate business.

Tax Considerations: Independent contractors are considered self-employed, which means they are responsible for paying both the employer and employee portions of Social Security and Medicare taxes. It's crucial to set aside funds for taxes and potentially work with an accountant to manage your financial affairs. Confirm with your tax advisor to get clarity on how this might impact your business.

Employee

Structured Work Environment: As an employee of a real estate brokerage, you typically operate within a more structured and regulated environment. You may have set working hours, office space provided by the brokerage, and a clear chain of command.

Steady Salary or Hourly Pay: Employees often receive a regular salary or hourly wage, providing more financial stability compared to the commission-based income of independent contractors. Some brokerages may also offer bonuses or incentives for achieving specific goals.

Limited Business Expenses: Unlike independent contractors, employees may not have to worry about covering many business expenses, as these are often shouldered by the brokerage.

Tax Simplification: Employees have taxes withheld from their paychecks, simplifying the tax process. You won't be responsible for paying the employer portion of Social Security and Medicare taxes, as the brokerage takes care of this.

Which Is Right for You?

The choice between being an independent contractor and an employee depends on your preferences, career goals, broker affiliation, or job in real estate. Independent contracting offers more freedom and the potential for higher earnings. However, it also entails greater financial risk and responsibility. Being an employee provides stability and may be preferable if you want a more structured work environment and a consistent income.

Ultimately, it's crucial to discuss your options with potential brokerages and consider your career objectives when deciding which classification aligns best with your aspirations in the real estate industry.

Chapter Fourteen

Connections vs. Relationships

Since social media, many people misconstrue following for relationships. And...although a substantial social media following strokes the ego and can come in handy, those that follow (or are connected) are not necessarily your relationships. However, they are people you are socially connected to aka your audience and the opportunity to build relationships and do business with at least some of your audience, is possible.

Connections are people you know, however not necessarily a relationship. Relationships require connection but are basically people you know or know of. People you know of, are people you have a one-way connection with, you know of them through a mutual relationship, but that connection does not know of you or vice versa. Good relationships or at least the type I am referring to encompass a two-way connection, fondness, and trust and require some work.

Understanding how to cultivate and nurture good personal and professional relationships is a key component in the real estate business as an agent. Good relationships are the foundation of trust. Trust is developed over time through consistency and reliability. As a real estate agent, consistently delivering on your promises and commitments is key. Whether it's meeting deadlines, providing accurate information, or being responsive to client inquiries, demonstrating reliability helps instill confidence in your clients. Individuals with whom you've forged good relationships will often know, like, and trust you enough to do business with you. And that, in short, is your sphere of influence (SOI).

More of My Story It's definitely the relationships for me! Throughout my dynamic career which has spanned over several industries, leadership positions, and businesses, the relationships I've formed led to some of my greatest wins. Actually, all of my real estate deals to date have culminated from a relationship I've built in one space or another. Stick with me, I'm making a connection. See what I did there!

My professional background, in the most succinct explanation, is business development. However, I've spent the bulk of my career and entrepreneurial ventures focused on non-profit organizational management with several organizations, including a consultant firm of my own. In the nonprofit leadership arena, developing the business, advancing the mission, and fundraising are integral parts of the job. Emphasis on fundraising! One of the most effective ways to get good at fundraising is to get good at building strategic relationships. And the very same application is true for a real estate agent who wants to be successful in real estate.

My Career Switch to Real Estate

Why the switch to real estate? Technically, real estate wasn't exactly an "or" for me. I haven't left the non-profit sector as I continue to consult and lead organizations through board representation and volunteer work. In fact, at the moment of writing this book, I serve as president of a chamber of commerce and vice president of a non-profit educational excellence fund. Yet, as a licensed agent and owner (Senior Vice President and Chief Operating Officer) of a real estate brokerage, I get to continue utilizing my business development skill-set to educate and empower agents and clients to achieve their strategic goals, elevate their lifestyles, enhance their businesses and real estate aspirations while doing many of the things I enjoy, like building relationships!

For you, as you navigate the real estate industry, understand that relationships are necessary. You are either going to start with the relationships you have, known as your sphere of influence (SOI), or you'll focus on building them to start your business. Even if you are new to an area with no friends or family you can build relationships and create an SOI. And..there are other ways to build and announce your real estate business outside of your current relationships, so if you don't currently have an SOI stay encouraged.

Don't worry, **YOU GOT THIS!**

Pro Tip: Aside from participating in local events, volunteering presents an excellent avenue for building relationships. Seek out opportunities within your community and market that match your skills, lifestyle, or business interests. Consider contributing to food pantries, getting involved with PTA activities, engaging with local churches, joining your Chamber of Commerce, participating in Rotary clubs, supporting the YMCA, connecting with art associations, or even getting involved in local sports leagues and other local non-profit organizations. Identify what you can bring to the table and always prioritize adding value to the causes and communities you engage with.

Chapter Fifteen

Embracing The Power of Your Sphere of Influence

Your Sphere of Influence, more sexily known as SOI can be a dynamic weapon in your real estate business if you use it well. It can take your business from "cute" to "fire" or aka idea to success. As a real estate agent, recognizing the significance of your SOI is fundamental to excelling in this industry. Dominating a market could directly hinge on your effectiveness in cultivating and leveraging your SOI. Embracing what it is, why it holds such importance, and how you can leverage its benefits are key factors in propelling your real estate career and business forward faster and in many cases, with less effort.

And guess what? Even though it will expand over time; before you begin your career and start your real estate business, you already have a sphere! How? There is definitely at least one person who knows likes and trusts you somewhere and I bet if you strategically thought about it, you could identify several.

Sphere of Influence Demystified

Your SOI represents the network of individuals with whom you have personal or professional relationships. These relationships can include family members, friends, acquaintances, colleagues, past clients, neighbors, and even those you interact with on social media. When you have a strong SOI, your SOI might also include the connections or relationships of those within your SOI. Your people's-people can become your people too when they need and learn about your services.

Why Your Sphere Matters

Essentially, your SOI is so powerful because it's a web of relationships that you can tap into for various purposes, including building your real estate business. Your SOI is not just another list of contacts; it's a valuable asset that can significantly impact your real estate career in numerous ways.

Trust and Credibility: Your SOI consists of people who know you, trust you, and have confidence in your abilities. This pre-existing trust can make it easier to establish yourself as a credible real estate professional.

Referral Potential: Your SOI can be a consistent source of referrals. When individuals in your network need real estate services or know someone who is, they are more likely to recommend you due to the trust you've built with them.

Do you get it? Your sphere is rooting for you. They are like having a personal fan club! Go ahead celebrity, get outside, and Go...off!

Cost-Effective Marketing: Marketing to your SOI is often more cost-effective than targeting strangers because your SOI has already warmed up to you whereas strangers will take longer to defrost. Studies show that It takes about 7-13 touches before a stranger might warm up to hiring you as their agent. However, with your SOI, you have a competitive edge. Your existing connections are more receptive to your messages, reducing the need for extensive advertising and prospecting.

Market Insights: Your SOI can provide valuable insights into local market conditions and trends. Although I wouldn't solely rely on their information as it can sometimes offer bias, their perspectives can inform some of your business decisions and strategies. Their perspectives can also help you sort out the information you are finding in the data you pull.

Repeat Business: Clients who have closed transactions with you previously are part of your SOI. In addition to the referral business they may offer, they can become repeat customers for future transactions. Fostering long-term relationships is essential for sustainable success. Keep in touch with your clients after you close their transactions.

Personalized Approach: You have a deeper understanding of your SOI's needs, preferences, and motivations. You know more about them than you know about a stranger. You have some inclinations about their likes, dislikes, and life changes. This knowledge allows you to tailor your services and communication to better serve them.

Pro Tip: The National Association of Realtors conducted a study that shows over 50% of an average agent's real estate business comes from repeat and referral business. That means that you have 50% of your lead generating in "the bag" just by executing good systems that help you keep in touch with ease! And...to drive this point home, NAR studies also show that the top reason almost 90% of clients decided to work with a different agent on their next transaction was because they had not heard from their agent since closing. Keep in touch with all of your sphere to ensure they don't forget that you are their preferred real estate expert.

Building and Expanding Your Sphere of Influence

Your Sphere of Influence is not static; it's a relationship entity that you can nurture, expand, and evolve. Check out these ideas on how to build and grow your SOI:

Who You Know: Begin by listing all the individuals you know personally or professionally. This can include family, friends, former colleagues, schoolmates, and more. If you are drawing a blank, take a look at your phone, email, and social media contacts. Keep your sphere in the loop of your accomplishments in real estate. Start with something simple like informing them that you've started a new business venture in real estate and or recently passed your real estate exam.

Leverage Technology: Social media platforms like LinkedIn, Facebook, and Instagram can be powerful tools for expanding your SOI. Connect with individuals who align with your real estate business goals. Join groups to meet new people and use it as one of your many touch points with your SOI.

Pro Tip: Even as someone who is not licensed yet and considering getting into real estate, you can join many real estate business groups to build relationships, so get started.

Engage in Networking: Attend industry events, local community gatherings, and networking functions. Stewarding your relationships during face-to-face engagements can deepen your SOI.

Offer Value: As a matter of fact, lead with value as a rule. To maintain and expand your SOI, consistently provide value to your connections. Share informative real estate content, offer assistance, and stay engaged.

Ask for Referrals: People who know like and trust you want to know how they can help you win. Tell them! Don't hesitate to ask your current SOI members for referrals or introductions to others in their network who may benefit from your services.

Nurture Relationships: Building your SOI isn't a one-time effort; it requires ongoing relationship management. Stay in touch with them, remember their important dates, check in, and offer assistance when needed.

More of My Story When I started my real estate business I had to inform my SOI of my new venture and in a crafty way to eliminate confusion. In short, my SOI mostly knew that my professional space was focused on business development for nonprofit organizations. It was important to me that my SOI was aware that I added real estate to my professional landscape. Initially, I used all of the free tools that I had available including email, phone, text and you guessed it, all of my social media profiles to build awareness about my business.

Social media worked well. My sphere happily celebrated my new business on their pages. Although I believe many of them would have done it anyway, I know they shared because I asked. Additionally, as word got around to people whom I hadn't shared my business with yet, I found myself tagged in several of my SOI's posts. It wasn't long before I started getting calls. I think one of my favorites was from an elementary school classmate whom I hadn't connected with since the 3rd grade!

Stay Top of Mind

Maintaining communication with your Sphere of Influence is pivotal to igniting its power for your business. It's one of the easiest things you need to do in your business. Here are effective strategies to stay connected:

Regular Updates: Send out newsletters, emails, or social media updates that share valuable real estate insights, market updates, and tips. In addition, encourage your SOI to share and celebrate your accomplishments.

Personal Touch: Don't underestimate the power of personalized messages. Send handwritten notes for special occasions or simply reach out to check in. Sometimes it's the little things that keep you in someone's memory bank.

Appreciation Events: Host events or gatherings to show your appreciation for your SOI. These events can strengthen relationships and foster goodwill. Host a holiday event or a game night and invite your sphere. At the end of the event give all of your attendees a "swag" bag with goodies and your business card or another branded item.

Social Media Engagement: Stay active on your social media platforms by engaging with comments, sharing relevant content, and participating in discussions. In addition to engagement, don't forget to post. Share a blend of real estate-related and fun personal content so you don't come off as "spammy"

Client Recognition: Acknowledge your clients' achievements and milestones, such as birthdays, anniversaries, and home purchase anniversaries.

Maintaining Professionalism and Trust

As you engage with your SOI, it's crucial to maintain professionalism and build trust. Professionalism might sound odd for the portion of your SOI that happens to be your first cousin or best friend who knows many intricate or intimate details about your life. However, when dealing with their real estate transactions and or discussing your real estate business, maintain a high level of professionalism that they can count on. It will help those who have seen you in your superhero pajamas take your business seriously and those who don't know you as intimately hold your services at a high level. It will help you increase or strengthen your sphere of influence.

Regardless of who you are engaging with in your SOI, check out these key principles to uphold to showcase professionalism and build trust.

Honesty and Transparency: Trust is built on integrity so be honest in your dealings and transparent in your communication. During the transaction, keep your client up to date and informed about the process. Effective communication is essential for trust-building and plays a pivotal role in your real estate business success.

Confidentiality: Respect your client's privacy and maintain the confidentiality of sensitive information. Be sure to adhere to your fiduciary responsibility when it comes to confidentiality.

Consistency: Consistently deliver exceptional service and follow through on your commitments. Reliability builds trust.

Problem Resolution: Address any issues or conflicts promptly and professionally. How you handle challenges can impact trust. And definitely keep your clients well informed of the issue and the progress of its resolution.

Referrals: The Lifeblood of Your SOI

Referrals are the lifeblood of your SOI. It's the gift that keeps giving. Here's how to encourage and handle them effectively:

Educate Your SOI: Ensure your connections understand the types of referrals you're seeking and the qualities of your ideal clients. This helps them provide more targeted referrals. For example, if your target clients are seniors looking to downsize or new business owners seeking a commercial lease, make that clear.

Ask for Referrals: Make it a standard practice to ask your SOI members for referrals. If they've had a positive experience working with you, they'll likely be happy to recommend your services. Close mouths don't get fed so don't assume that someone in your SOI will refer you just because they know you. Ask!

Stay in Touch: Keep your referrers updated on the general progress of the referrals they've provided. This reinforces their trust in your professionalism. A simple thank you note, call, or text to confirm that you connected with their referral is sufficient, just leave out the confidential details. Remember that confidentiality is a fiduciary responsibility so do not reveal any confidential information.

Express Gratitude: Always express your gratitude when receiving referrals. A simple thank-you note or gesture can go a long way in nurturing these important relationships. Remember that your SOI is routing for you to win so they usually aren't looking for anything more than a verbal thank you. However, a handwritten note would leave a nice impression.

Benefits of a Robust Sphere of Influence

A well-cultivated and nurtured SOI offers several business-boosting benefits.

Increased Business: A strong SOI can be a consistent source of new clients and referrals, leading to increased business opportunities.

Enhanced Reputation: Your reputation as a trustworthy and reliable real estate professional will grow within your community and industry.

Professional Growth: Building your SOI requires honing essential networking and relationship-building skills, which can foster your professional growth.

Sustainable Success: A robust Sphere of Influence can provide a steady stream of business, ensuring your long-term success in the real estate industry.

Nurture Your Sphere, Prosper in Real Estate

Your Sphere of Influence is more than just a list of contacts; it's a dynamic network of relationships that can drive your real estate career and business to new heights. By understanding its importance, continually expanding it, and nurturing the connections within it, you can harness the power of your SOI to build a thriving and sustainable real estate business.

Chapter Sixteen

Real Estate Agent To Be or Not To Be?

Since you are nearing the end of this book, you most likely have a good idea if this industry makes sense for you. However, proper planning and a realistic view of this business before you leap in will be your superpower. I enjoy offering value to others through real estate. There are so many intriguing spaces in this industry that I'm passionate about and align with my strategic goals and I'm sure you'll find your lane too.

Is becoming a real estate agent or a referral agent the right fit for you? Dig deep because that is a question only you can answer. And honestly, there is no rush because the test for both is exactly the same. Take time to realistically consider if your capacity will enable you to offer what it takes to achieve your desired level of success.

Income Variability

Think about the income variability and if you have the capacity in your budget to handle large gaps in time before you get paid. Remember that most real estate agents are independent contractors. This means you won't receive compensation on a dependable or consistent basis or at least not until you build your business to that extent.

Remember that no matter how much you make, or when you make it, you'll have mandatory business expenses. Planning those expenses in your budget at the onset, before you start will set you up for sustainability.

Independence

As a real estate agent, you are the business and every element of the business is your responsibility. Consider your comfort level with working independently even if you are affiliated with a broker. A real estate agent who is an independent contractor (affiliated with a broker or not) will need to create systems, execute tasks, generate new business, and manage their schedule on their own. Your ability to stay organized and self-motivated will be critical as a real estate agent.

People Skills

People skills are an area you won't escape as a real estate agent. It's hard to get around dealing with people so think about how well you manage working with people and different personalities. The transaction process can be filled with emotions which can heighten tension which you'll at times need to de-escalate. On the other hand, you'll gain new relationships over time which means you'll have plenty of people rooting for you and desiring you to be their real estate BFF.

Resilience and Patience

The real estate business is financially lucrative and intrinsically rewarding, yet full of rejection. No matter how efficient and organized you are, there will be delays and setbacks beyond your control. Stay in the business long enough and you'll come across transactions that were perfectly aligned to close, that won't after you put in an abundance of work. Resilience and patience are necessary attributes with a touch of grace and the ability to pause and count yourself to ten.

Life Long Learning

If success is in your plan as a real estate agent, learning for life should be too. The real estate business evolves and you'll need to stay on top of it, daily. Understanding your market won't be a one-and-done. It's a practice, something you need to do often. Technology will change and you'll need to know how to use it. Meet an agent in the business long enough and you'll hear how email, cell phones, texting, social media, or AI didn't exist when they started their career. Your willingness for continuous learning will be your leverage because surprisingly many agents skip that part. Additionally, the idea that marketing is a necessary component, is one of those areas in the real estate business that catches some agents off guard. If marketing is not already your strength, consider your capacity to learn the basics.

At the end of the day, if you really love the idea of getting into real estate but don't think becoming an agent is on your horizon, there are many other options. Maybe real estate developing or mortgage brokering are for you or skipping the tests altogether and becoming an investor instead!

If you are still unsure, I know this amazing licensed real estate professional, multi-real estate real estate brokerage owner, seasoned entrepreneur, and author who offers "Pick My Brain" one-on-one consultation sessions. The sessions are designed for current and prospective real estate professionals.

Scan the QR code below to schedule a session with me. Pssst...unlike the others, this QR code is different from the code in other chapters so you'll want to scan this one to schedule a session.

Remember the secret go-pro sauce.

Learn continuously. Lead with undeniable value. Grow unapologetically. Repeat.

Chapter Seventeen

Unleash Your Real Estate Journey with Confidence and Passion!

Congratulations, future real estate agent and business mogul. Kudos to you for taking a step toward becoming a successful real estate agent! You've almost reached the end of this book and, most likely, the beginning of your successful real estate business!

Overall, becoming a real estate agent can be a fulfilling and financially rewarding career choice. With the ability to earn a lot of money, have autonomous flexibility in your schedule, the satisfaction of personal growth, and helping people fulfill their real estate aspirations, what's not to love? If you're interested in pursuing a career in real estate, by now you have probably determined that it's definitely worth considering!

At this point, you've absorbed the wisdom and insights, and you're armed with the knowledge needed to step into this dynamic real estate industry. Embrace your passion for this business and allow it to thrust you to the top! Yet, stay humble and proactively practice responding with grace. This business, as lovely as it is, will dually reward you abundantly while testing your inner limits. Real estate is primarily a beautiful career, but it would be a fallacy if I didn't share that it can be both a beauty and a beast.

Although becoming a real estate agent is a leap into something new, it is not a sprint. It is not all the glitz, glamour, cute suits, and high heels you see on reality shows or your local neighborhood agents' social feeds. The real estate business is not always graceful, as it will go high and low. Literally and figuratively, multiple times within the same transaction.

Soak it up, enjoy every milestone, learn from every experience, and continue to fuel your passion. The sheer joy of helping people find their dream homes and business spaces, the satisfaction of sealing deals, and the sense of accomplishment when you overcome challenges will make every effort worthwhile. When you face rejection, embrace those L's, the love of learning, and why not...go ahead and laugh too. Your success is always within your reach only if you stretch and grab it.

Believe that you are designed for greatness, and success is just in you! Know that you have what it takes to create a legacy, build wealth for yourself and others, develop a thriving business, and impact the lives of countless individuals if you gather your plans and execute them like a pro even when you don't feel like one.

You read, you thought, you absorbed and now it's time to execute.

The fastest way to reach your goals is to start. Let's Go...take your next step!

All the best to you on your remarkable journey as a real estate agent!

P.S. Don't forget your secret go-pro sauce...

LEARN CONTINUOUSLY. LEAD WITH UNDENIABLE VALUE. GROW UNAPOLOGETICALLY. REPEAT.

For additional guidance on becoming a real estate agent, check out the **HEY...FUTURE REAL ESTATE AGENT: PRO PLANNER**. It offers study guides, worksheets, checklists, and business plan prep tools to mentor your path into the real estate business and beyond with success. If you scan and get our coming soon message, just sign up for the waiting list and I'll let you know once it's on the market. I promise....it's already written!

Pssst...this QR code is different from the others.

Thanks for Reading!

HEY... FUTURE REAL ESTATE AGENT

YOUR STRATEGIC GUIDE INTO THE BUSINESS AND BEYOND

BY DESIREE L. BURGOS

Rate & Review Please

THE HIGHEST COMPLIMENT IS YOUR 5-STAR RATING AND REVIEW

Tell us how you enjoyed the book

Scan me

- STUDY BRAIN CHEATS
- STUDY RESOURCES
- EQUIPMENT LIST
- CRM SUGGESTIONS
- PICK MY BRAIN CONSULTATION LINK
- HEY...FUTURE REAL ESTATE AGENT PRO PLANNER LINK
- REAL ESTATE APPAREL STORE
- 12 MONTH BUDGET WORKSHEETS

www.ingramcontent.com/pod-product-compliance
Lightning Source LLC
LaVergne TN
LVHW010948110826
845149LV00015B/3268

* 9 7 9 8 9 8 9 8 7 8 8 1 9 *